Reimagining the Educated Mind

Reimagining the Educated Mind

Using Student Choice Curriculum to Transform Educational Practices

Ben Graffam

ROWMAN & LITTLEFIELD
Lanham • Boulder • New York • London

Published by Rowman & Littlefield
An imprint of The Rowman & Littlefield Publishing Group, Inc.
4501 Forbes Boulevard, Suite 200, Lanham, Maryland 20706
www.rowman.com

6 Tinworth Street, London SE11 5AL, United Kingdom

Copyright © 2019 by Ben Graffam

All rights reserved. No part of this book may be reproduced in any form or by any electronic or mechanical means, including information storage and retrieval systems, without written permission from the publisher, except by a reviewer who may quote passages in a review.

British Library Cataloguing in Publication Information Available

Library of Congress Cataloging-in-Publication Data Is Available
ISBN 978-1-4758-4887-8 (cloth: alk. paper)
ISBN 978-1-4758-4888-5 (pbk: alk. paper)
ISBN 978-1-4758-4889-2 (electronic)

∞™ The paper used in this publication meets the minimum requirements of American National Standard for Information Sciences—Permanence of Paper for Printed Library Materials, ANSI/NISO Z39.48–1992.

To the man who taught me more than anyone,
and who gave me my first basketball.
This is for you, Dad.

Contents

Foreword ix
Chris Unger

Preface xv

Acknowledgments xix

Introduction 1

1 Learning with a Purpose 9
2 Linking Academics with Interest 25
3 Student Choice within the Curriculum 53
4 Putting the Program into Practice 87
5 The Learning Environments 111
6 Education Is Democratic 131

Selected Bibliography 145

About the Author 147

Foreword

WHY CAN'T WE MOVE FORWARD?

No one can argue that the way we envision teaching and learning is fundamentally stuck inside a paradigm of how we see "schooling." Lots of kids in a building—sometimes a very large building—working with and moving in groups from one individual teacher or another with a clearly limited focus on certain expected content and skills. And this is how we "educate." And as Ben so plainly makes clear throughout this book, it cuts against the grain of what we know about transformative learning.

We know that we are built to learn. In reality, we, including our youth and adolescents, are social animals with a disposition to explore and figure things out, through conversation, play, and activity. But we can't move forward because in most cases we are stuck in the image of schooling we have always known and continue to perpetuate, focused on the absorption of content more so than the development of valuable skills and dispositions such as creativity, personal sensemaking, ingenuity, and agency.

IMAGES OF POSSIBILITY

Thankfully, there are a few who have ventured forth and have reimagined the way we could think about teaching and learning, as well as schooling. And, thankfully, we have voices like Ben's who can help us to see the need for revisioning our perspective of teaching, learning, and schooling. What is impacted when we see, hear, and read about these alternatives to teaching, learning, and schooling as we now know it? First, the design of our schools. Bigger and smaller spaces for collaboration and private work should be the norm (such as makerspaces, design studios, and community engagement), not thirty students sitting facing a chalkboard routinely taking notes or attempting to memorize information from a text. We now know from a few amazing and school-stretching programs that learning in the *real world* is the best form of learning. We know from years of cognitive science—and, frankly, pure common sense—that the best learning is authentic, meaning the student *cares* about it and it has meaningful application in the world.

Let me share just a few of these examples that you yourself can go see and begin to appreciate the very real connection between what Ben calls out for as a new modality for thinking about teaching, learning, and schooling and these two communities where this modality is certainly alive and well and the heartbeat of their success.

IOWA BIG, CEDAR RAPIDS, IOWA

Iowa BIG is only four years old, with 180 high school students from three different school districts in the area. As a student, you can go full-time or part-time, for example, taking math and foreign language at your home high school in the morning and then traveling to Iowa BIG in the afternoon. The space for convening in teams or as a school is the bottom floor of a start-up building, which includes a number of other small businesses trying to make a go of it. It's a large space with several other smaller spaces to work independently or in small groups, with some other side rooms for group meetings and conversation.

There are no classes and no classrooms . . . unless the students ask for them. Students are not driven by an external curriculum of content but an authentic curriculum of real-world, community-based projects that need to get done! And I don't mean "make-believe" projects like building a bridge out of Popsicle sticks, gumdrops, and straws. But *real* projects.

For example, one group of students has been working with the United Way of East Central Iowa to assess the level of trauma-informed practices in the Cedar Rapids area to inform the work of school, nonprofits, and law enforcement. Another group of students uses modeling software to map stormwater runoff in the greater Marion Uptown district of Cedar Rapids as it moves from the streets through the man-made and natural drainage systems of the community, aiming to identify and track the flow of pollutants eventually impacting the Uptown Marion/Donnelly Park sub-watershed.

Say what? What are these projects? How is it the students come to be working on them? How are they working in the community? Simple. The students and teachers (facilitators) at Iowa BIG started by going to for-profits, nonprofits, and government agencies in their community and asked this simple question: "Do you have a project that really needs to get done but you are just too busy to get to?" Typically, organizations have a lot of these. "And, if so, since you can't get to it, do you mind if five or six of our students take a whack at it?" So, perhaps this is not the exact language used, but the point is that over time the school has begun to collect lots and lots of potential community-based projects. And then the students look into this "project pool," as they call it, and then decide what they would like to work on. From there, teams of students, with an advisor, work with the community organization to clarify the need, identify a desired result, and then get busy.

Over a year ago, another group of students went to an architecture firm with the same question: Do you have a project that you need to get done but you are simply just too busy right now to get to it? Yes, we have been hired to design a $1.3 million pedestrian footbridge to go over the river. But we can't get to it for six months. Too busy with other projects right now. "Fine," the advisor said. "Would you mind if five or six of our students take a whack at it?" Two months later, the students returned to the architecture firm not only with the bridge engineered but with an artistic display of etched glass that would be a part of the bridge so that as you walked across the river it would look as if birds were fluttering along by you.

Last I heard, this bridge was one of three designs up for consideration by the city council.

Are these kids learning anything? You bet! They are learning engineering, computer modeling, marketing, social service, finances, entrepreneurship, aquaponic farming, data analysis, research, and so on. But the biggest things they may be learning are: What am I interested in? What do I like doing? What am I good at? What might I want to pursue further? How does a team work best? How can I make a difference in the world?

BLUE VALLEY CENTER FOR ADVANCED PROFESSIONAL STUDIES

The Blue Valley Center for Advanced Professional Studies (BVCAPS; bvcaps.yourcapsnetwork.org) is a profession-based high school program on steroids in Overland Park, Kansas. Like Iowa BIG, students can go part-time or full-time during their junior and senior years.

Different from Iowa BIG, BVCAPS provides learning opportunities across six different predefined industry strands: bioscience, business technology and media, engineering, human services, medicine and health care, and entrepreneurship. But much like Iowa BIG, the work at BVCAPS is comprised of real-world projects connected to industry and partners. But in addition, they offer "classes," which run far more like workshops, and are geared toward an industry partner or a real-world-driven project.

When I visited the program, I met with the VetMed students, who were running an actual farm and learning about farm husbandry. The life-size, rubber model of a cow's uterus is where the VetMed students rehearsed the delivery of a calf—an undertaking I personally have never tried. These students were also raising chickens, pigs, horses, and a few other animals. But before you say "How nice, they run a farm," the facilitator of this group pressed students to explore specific issues of veterinary medicine that matter to them. One student, for example, shared that she took a deep dive into "old dog vestibular syndrome," which is a condition that causes dogs to be perpetually dizzy caused by an inner-ear imbalance. Why would she study such a thing? "Because my dog got it, so I wanted to understand what was happening to her." Another student investigated the effects of secondhand smoke on the lungs and nasal cavities of animals. Why? "Because my dad is a smoker and I have had several dogs who have died of cancer in the lungs and nasal cavities."

Another pair of students I met were working in the bioscience strand. Why? They like to figure out things and were interested in finding solutions to help people. Turns out Neeha and Hannah were doing original molecular research at the BVCAPS facility, mentored by a research scientist at the University of Kansas medical school and Johns Hopkins, respectively. Upon asking, I learned that Neeha was looking at the "CRISPR decaps 9 system" and "how I could use that system to design antibiotic-resistant cells not resistant to antibiotics anymore." Direct quote. For Hannah, she was investigating signal pathways involved with liver fibrosis.

What does it mean for students to pursue what *they* are interested in? To be "making, creating, and doing" something that is relevant to them and has real-world impact? At BVCAPS it means making a movie, designing a hugging machine for autistic youth, developing new foods, creating an entrepreneurial business, learning how to take care of patients. As one student said, "We are able to decide what we are studying, because everybody figures out what they are passionate about and then gears their entire project toward pursuing that passion. So it is something a traditional classroom would not provide us with. [We have] the flexibility to figure out what we are interested in and then make our entire experience around that interest."

THIS BOOK

The factory is broken. And as much as we tinker with what teaching, learning, and schooling looks like, for the most part we are just painting the wall or adding some different furniture to the house. We are not substantively changing *what* the school, teaching, and learning looks like. Schools for the most part look like and are run like one another. We see classrooms, coverage of siloed and decontextualized subjects, a single teacher with a group of students, time governed through short bursts of lecture or small-group or individual activity, learning completely disconnected from actual student interest and real-world activity.

As I am prone to say: There are cool schools here and there . . . but there should be cool schools everywhere. If an educator community were able to start from scratch, I would pay attention to what is in Ben's book. And even if you aren't wanting to or can start from scratch, you can begin to think of ways to expand student choice for far greater student engagement, which ultimately leads to deeper student learning. If we could do a better job focusing on these things, and learning from one another on how to do so, we would have more than just some cool schools here and there but possibly more cool schools everywhere, providing greater opportunity for all students and our communities.

Dr. Chris Unger
Associate Teaching Professor
Network of Experiential Learning Educators
Graduate School of Education
Northeastern University
Boston, Massachusetts

Preface

The history of science tells us that that Albert Einstein developed a good deal of his general and special theories of relativity through a thought experiment he carried out when he was in his mid-teens. Intrigued with light and speed, he asked himself what it would be like to sit on a beam of light, traveling at that speed. What might he see?

One theory was that he might see all sides of an object at the same time, not just the side which was facing him, since, he conjectured, light travels so rapidly, it hits all open sides of every proximal object at almost exactly the same time, perhaps with mildly different intensities. Another theory posited that traveling at the speed of light would change the nature of "now" as it is normally understood. Two people, by nature of their locations, would see two lightning strikes differently, one seeing them as simultaneous and the other seeing a mild lag in time between the strikes.

As these and other speculations from his famous thought experiments evolved into his theories on relativity, Einstein changed the world as we knew it. Time and again a variety of experiments in physics have shown his insights to be spot on. We credit him with many things, but to me, one of the biggest is that Einstein's thought experiments got people talking about the often incomprehensible match between what we believe and what really exists in the world we inhabit. Humans have spent lots of cognitive time accepting what appears to be common sense, when other explanations better suit particular phenomena.

Those conversations, shared by laypeople and scientists alike, changed the nature of science and knowledge, as talk engendered opportunities to understand more fully that which had been taken for granted, and often for the wrong reasons. As an educator, I know only too well how held beliefs can serve as obstacles to a student's learning, and part of my job must focus on supplying reasons for a student to question what has, heretofore, been believed. Many times that practice includes encouraging that student to create some thought experiments of her own.

Though perhaps not as grand as Einstein's riding that beam of light, this book represents outcomes of one of my ongoing thought experiments on the nature of education. I often asked myself, "What would happen to education if we allowed students to choose not only the subjects they studied but also the way they were taught and evaluated?" In these days of standardized tests and core curricula, this is somewhat controversial, as it changes the form and direction of institutional education as we understand it. But perhaps, I thought, educators have clung to a common-sense notion, when other explanations better suit how education should work.

This thought experiment allowed me to imagine a student who had chosen basketball for the daily engagements she might experience at her high school. Because she has a love for the game, she and her teachers would use the sport to study history, math, literature, science, the arts, and foreign languages. Through shared conversations with her teachers and other students, this student would cobble together a plethora of goals and methods for demonstrating a qualified set of outcomes in each subject area that would ultimately allow the school to grant her the privileges of graduation.

My thought experiment also persuaded me to imagine a school that dignified choices of this type, a school made up of different learning spaces where different kinds of learning engagements occurred on a daily basis. Included in this was the assembling of many authentic audiences, community members who would work with teachers and students, sharing their life experiences in the learning process. It was, to some degree, student-centered learning on steroids. But I knew it was more than that. I came to call the program Student Choice Curriculum.

It began to make a lot of sense to me.

Education is the most important process of a democratic nation. As democracy's inclusionary structure expands, the need for an educated population intensifies. More possibilities in life require greater critical applications from citizens. Moreover, the critical thought necessary to unpack the myriad manifestations of freedom and equality that make up democracy must be derived from a multiplex of human experiences. In other words, it takes smart people to have a successful democracy. Education must then be robust.

Of course, it is not just a collection of facts that makes up this kind of robust intelligence. Rather, successful democracies—perhaps all technological societies—need citizens who are flexible with their learning, able to see and imagine various positive outcomes, and keen at both problem-solving and the more important problem-finding. In the thought experiment that frames this book, I explore ways these ends might be achieved in schools that put student choice of topic, method, and evaluation front and center.

It is, for sure, very difficult to determine what a proper education ought to entail. Time and place play significant roles. In technological America, students need significant doses of math, science, and the humanities, but from what perspective? Toward what end do we aim our curricula? What are the learning experiences that matter to each individual learner? My thought experiment led me to understand that while it may be difficult to determine proper education, it is delightful to imagine it, to detail the nuances, and to let students think freely through the new learning spaces.

Conventional wisdom accepts that it is not mere information that matters most in a complex world, not the theories that define various fields of study; rather it is the interconnection each individual learner makes with the process of learning, the highly personal fit that occurs between wanting to and ultimately being able to know something. In minds as young as those we teach in K–12 schools, it is not the information a student is taught that provides the necessary elements of an educated mind; it is the how and the why and the wherefore supporting that information that make learning valuable.

My thought experiment allowed me to explore myriad aspects of education as it is currently functioning, and then to tweak, change, and jettison many of these in the service of that experiment. I began to see how allowing choice shifts the responsibility of learning, and that such a shift bestows benefits upon the learner, mainly because she would now be engaged internally and interactively toward an end she saw to be valuable. Personal energy was employed working on personal problems that she could solve because she *wanted* to solve them.

This is the largest idea this book addresses, that education must be based on the desires, the inquiries, and the experiences of the learner. In dignifying students' choices, Student Choice Curriculum teaches students how to learn. We are, sad to say, not doing a good job of this in our schools. As I have worked in classrooms since 1982, teaching a broad assortment of high school students, I have seen education's continued march in the opposite direction. The graduating class of 2018 will be recognized as the most-tested group of students our country has produced . . . until the graduating class of 2019.

It doesn't have to be this way. If, as a culture, we could imagine new educational paradigms; different ways to dignify the process of learning, and develop alternative, community-driven elements of evaluation, much might be accomplished for our learners and our democracy. In trying not just to complain about things gone wrong—something teachers can do pretty well—I thought it better to offer a solution that might somehow engender some significant conversations about the problem. So I wrote this book.

Like Einstein's insights from riding a beam of light, I hope this thought experiment engenders various conversations among educators, parents, legislators, and, of course, students, not only about Student Choice Curriculum but also about how to improve education in America. Much is not proceeding well in the formal educational environments in our country. Certain battle lines have been drawn in the debate of what should be done. Sides are forming. Clearly, something must change. Student Choice Curriculum is my entry into the fray.

Acknowledgments

It is one thing to feel the pleasure when your words find their way into a published work, quite another to know how that would not have happened without the support, encouragement, and guidance of many friends and colleagues. Lots of people played a role here, and I am most grateful for those who read all or parts of the text and then offered criticisms, corrections, suggestions, and even arguments for what appears on these pages.

I am thankful for the early input of Susan Truett, Julie Ward, and Dr. Gwen Kessell, all educators of significant skill. Susan is vice president of the board of directors for a local Montessori school; she is also its cofounder. She has a keen sense for seeing the student when everyone else seems to be seeing the system. Julie is principal at Rochelle School of the Arts, a public school where students set some of their own goals in their educational plans. And Gwen is the head of the lower school at All Saints Academy, a private school where she leads a cadre of teachers toward project-based learning experiences shaped and practiced by schools like High Tech High in San Diego, California.

I have also benefited tremendously from Dr. Jim Paul, professor emeritus, who guided me through my PhD program years ago at the University of South Florida (USF); Dr. Elizabeth Shaunessy-Dedrick, coordinator of USF's Gifted Education Program, with whom I shared several teaching engagements at USF; and Dr. Christine Weber, professor at the University of North Florida, with whom I worked on a Florida Department of Education Grant that reimagined and reworked the standards for gifted education in our state.

Jim's guidance and support, as always, was warm and challenging, and his critical input had a significant effect on this manuscript. Elizabeth's eye on the details of the text, especially those that described educational procedures, was perfect. Chris's work, as always, was theory laden, pushing for me to see other possibilities and alternative outcomes. Her questions let me know the conversations I hoped for could be started from this book. I am pleased to acknowledge their help and generosity.

Rob Riordan deserves kudos for connecting me with Dr. Chris Unger of Northeastern University, and thank you, Chris, for seeing enough in the words of a stranger to offer support and a wonderful foreword. And Tom Koerner, PhD, offered numerous insights and suggestions as my book went from submission to the productions department at Rowman & Littlefield. I had not been in this situation before, and without his guidance, I would not have found my way.

Other friends, though not directly involved in the text itself, offered constant encouragement about the project and prospect of this book. Thanks to Eddy Gonzales, Nick Johnston, Billy Lippy, and Steve Glick. Knowing that people in your inner circle support your creative experiments is always helpful and motivating.

Finally, to my wife, Cheryl, goes a busload of love, thanks, and appreciation. She's a wonderful educator, a gifted lab manager, and a perfect companion. When I needed advice she was there; when I needed space to write, she knew it; and when I didn't know what I needed, she did. I could not have persisted in this endeavor without her, not with this book, not with this life.

Introduction

Many years ago, I asked my students to participate in a project called Independent Homework. Twice a year, students would choose a topic or skill and spend self-selected time over an eight-week period developing expertise on that choice. At the end of the eight weeks, they would present their findings to their classmates, and in some situations, people of the community I could entice to attend. Students completed this work while we engaged in the other elements of our English class: Shakespeare, novels, and expository writing.

The parameters of the assignment required students to keep a learning log during the experience, reflecting on the problems and solutions they encountered along the way. In this log they recorded the questions that arose and the insights they may have discovered as they explored this new learning. I also met with each student twice during the eight-week period so I could keep up to speed on their progress.

While the work was independently selected, I asked for a preliminary proposal and explanation, in writing, of the topic, goals, and methods they chose. This was in case some of the work might be questioned by the school. I knew, for example, there would be pushback if a student experimented on a living creature or attempted to build a destructive device, and I accepted the responsibility of making sure none of that happened.

Generally, students responded energetically to the assignment, and a myriad of projects were proposed and carried out. Some students chose to explore proficiency in a new musical instrument; some attempted new methods of photography or other artistic expression; one learned not only how to crack a bullwhip, but also the many different techniques and purposes for making the whip crack. Another read *The Unabomber Manifesto*, attempting to understand the nature of Ted Kaczynski's rebellion. Many other projects filled the years this assignment ran in my classes.

It was a highly successful project, and something I believe my students enjoyed. Some, when I see them from time to time, still remind me of the work they did in their independent homework: learning how to pick locks or to juggle or to solve a Rubik's Cube, or to fathom the depths of human faith in the divine. In some ways, I have been writing this book for a long time, as my mind looked often for ways to include student interest in the work we explored in my classroom.

However, I adjusted my use of the assignment as school schedules tightened for state and national testing, and I found myself needing to fit into a smaller temporal space the "necessary" elements of a study of English. Initially, I shifted the assignment to only once per year, but as subsequent years took more time away from classroom practice, my teaching choices changed, and ultimately, independent homework disappeared from my pedagogical approach to high school English.

Some of these decisions were mine; but other changes were placed before me by administrators who were ensuring that our school would do well on the exams used to measure the quality of education we delivered. Education was not only becoming less student-centered, it was becoming less teacher-centered. Ask any working teacher of, say, twenty years' experience, and she will tell you how much her world has been changed by forces outside of education.

Thus, in other ways, the writing of this book is a recent occurrence, motivated by the changes and decisions that have incrementally influenced what schools can and should do.

These decisions have not been made, generally, by educators in the classroom, and, in nearly every way, I believe they have not moved the practice of education forward.

Schools of choice let parents decide where to enroll their children and why that school works for them. Market qualities determine which schools succeed and which don't. Options for relocating young learners to "better" schools appear annually. No longer do we attempt to make educational outcomes more effective in every school; today we label a school as "failing," and then allow parents to move their children away from that space. It is not a positive picture.

Thus, this book is my attempt to offer another option for school reform, focusing specific attention on the students' needs and interests. A few goals I hope to accomplish in this text are:

- To provide fodder for significant conversations about the role student choice should play in education
- To describe a process where the student plays a significant role in differentiating curriculum

- To explore the way normal human learning could be used to reshape educational paradigms
- To connect the process and outcomes of student choice to democratic principles

The basic structure of this book is nonlinear, whereby I present and then spiral back to the issues that, ultimately, will reveal the nature of Student Choice Curriculum. By the end, the reader will have explored age-old journalistic questions of who, what, when, where, why, and how, as well as seen certain examples of what I expect Student Choice Curriculum to look like. However, as I hope the book engenders rich conversations about the potential of this curriculum, little here should be taken as prescriptive. Readers should understand the text as mostly descriptive and suggestive, with the hope that it is also transformative.

Moreover, I suggest throughout the text that most of what makes student choice a plausible system for all school-based learners is already clear to most readers. Humans are learning machines. Our brains continually work to make meaning of our experiences, and when clear meaning doesn't present itself to us, we seek to find out why. We discern better ways to mow our lawns and to cook a soufflé. We investigate living wills and financial investments when the need arises. In short, we learn most often when we discern a needed skill or concept within the frameworks of how we live our lives.

Whether we are musicians, plumbers, hikers, advertisers, chefs, firefighters, or, yes, basketball players, we do the work necessary to learn how to be better at what we are and at what we love. A main argument of this book is that if this process works for humans in all walks of life, it should work for students in that walk of life. The book will take you through an assorted presentation of the ideas behind Student Choice Curriculum while simultaneously describing what such a school might look like.

Each chapter begins with some "Framing Thoughts," a set of suggestions, including questions and juxtapositions, for approaching the chapter. Each ends with a "Doubling Down on the Major Issues," a set of bulleted points that recap the important information of the chapter. I recognize that readers can make up their own minds about what the book is about and which are the major points, but, as stated, I do hope this text engenders some major conversations about education, so you may think of these two elements as seeds for the burgeoning talks.

Chapter 1 explores the role interest plays in human learning, suggesting that most people learn well what is derived from personal interests. Here I argue that in all walks of life it is a person's interest and particular needs that drive learning. When we find ourselves needing or wanting to be better at any set of particular skills or information, we dedicate personal time and energy toward that end. My experience tells me that all of us do this regularly, so a similar emphasis on personal interest would be a boon to classroom instruction.

Chapters 2 and 3 introduce Lindsey and three other hypothetical students used to detail parts of Student Choice Curriculum. Here I detail how an interest like basketball works as both an entry point and a significant exploratory method to the subjects generally required in high schools. History and mathematics take the lion's share of this description, but English, science, and the arts also receive attention.

Moreover, chapter 3 lays out some of the ways each year of a Student Choice Curriculum might be organized for three of the hypothetical students. Lindsey's choice of basketball, Anthony's exploration of music, and David's focus on the culinary arts are detailed in history, mathematics, English, science, and foreign languages. I don't suggest that what I offer would be the curriculum of the program as that would be a major contradiction to my goals of letting the students choose the path their learning should take. The offerings here are suggestions of possible ways the curriculum might be focused.

In chapter 4 the shifting paradigms that drive Student Choice Curriculum are detailed, especially the different learning relationships engendered between teachers and students. Education generally posits a teacher-student relationship as central to the learning process. Student Choice Curriculum will work from a learner-learner paradigm, asking both the teacher and the student to be heavily involved in creating and carrying out the curricular plan.

To some degree, this borrows from Paulo Freire, who claimed that in proper classrooms, teaching doesn't really occur, only learning. If we are to make important changes in our educational processes, something I truly hope for, we must rethink the role of the teacher in the learning process. Chapter 4 clarifies responsibilities for each role, the teacher and student, and it suggests how to begin such a program as a school-within-a-school concept.

Six differentiated learning spaces get the focus in chapter 5. It is my belief that a school's physical space must change significantly if we are to create education that matters. Student Choice Curriculum requires a different vision of schedules and learning spaces. Social Halls, Quiet Chambers, Studios, Quiet Study Centers, Collaborative Workspaces, and Interactive Construction Areas make up the reformed learning spaces of this program. The purpose of each is described here.

Chapter 6 concludes the book by arguing for democratizing education. Though I tried not to be overly political in the other chapters, I do believe our educational system has delivered to us the political incompetence we experience in America today. Student Choice Curriculum will allow a clearer juxtaposition of "freedom to" and "freedom from" as they function within educational paradigms. I don't believe our current system appreciates these freedoms at all.

Within that argument can be heard the necessary call for the freedom needed to be a good learner. Education cannot be forced on a person, even by coercion; rather it derives from a learner's needs. Democracy has promised a great deal to the citizens of our country. It is time those promises are kept for the students of our land. The chapter draws to a close by evoking Carl Sagan's desire that schools become places where students and teachers both learn how to learn.

Throughout, you'll see a basic plan of a school, as Student Choice Curriculum offers readers a chance to rethink how high school works. Ultimately, the reader should come away with an idea concrete enough to power the imagination and to engender collegial conversations about this kind of learning.

THE READERS

My wish is that two kinds of readers engage with this book. The first is the team of advocates for more student-centered learning in our schools. I hope Student Choice Curriculum helps stretch the goals of such advocacy to a new extent. I know many colleagues who wish for more opportunities to let students engage in deeper and broader personal explorations. There is a core of teachers who support much of what I offer here, and I hope they find this argument to their liking, not as ammunition but as creative methodology.

It is, however, to the other kind of reader that I direct the crux of my argument. This is the team of core-curricular, universal-standards people who understand education as inculcation, a top-down system where students attend school to glean necessary lessons only the wise and experienced know. This team believes schools can fail at the process of educating, and that when such failure occurs, parents should be allowed to move their children to other schools. This team has gained power over the years, and I hope they read my argument as intended, a way to improve educational practice and outcomes.

I believe most of the second team of readers are not teachers—though some clearly are. As a major goal of the book is to engender conversations about improving education, I hope both teams find this book to be a set of steps toward conversing with one another and not past one another. Dialogue, conversation, is a matter of creation, and it needs the careful, thoughtful input of many individuals. Education is important enough for these two teams (and others) to have materialized in the quest to bring about reform. Talking seriously about such reform is surely worth our efforts.

WHY BASKETBALL?

Before we get started, it is important to say why basketball serves as the learning interest in this book. Many alternative ideas could have served the same purpose, perhaps to a more accessible outcome. Why not guitar? Skateboarding? Aerodynamics? Any of those (and many more) would be acceptable as would the American Civil War, SCUBA diving, hiking, assassins, Chuck Berry, film noir, and on and on. The main claim of Student Choice Curriculum is that any topic ought to work.

So why basketball?

I love the game. When I was a high school kid, it was the only thing that mattered. I played whenever I could; I watched whenever I could; I thought about the game always. I slept with my ball; pictures of basketball players hung on my bedroom wall; there was a full court in my backyard where kids from all over our town came to play. I went into teaching initially so I could coach. I have always followed the game, most recently watching the Cavaliers defeat my beloved Celtics in Game 7 to move into the NBA finals.

But it's more than just my love for the game. Every high school has that cadre of students who walk around in the gear of their favorite team, who play on the school's varsity and JV squads, and who gather somewhere after school for pickup games. We stereotype those kids as dreamers who don't understand the odds of making a life in basketball, who won't do the work of getting an education so that when their playing days are over, they'll have something to fall back upon; we downgrade their love by informing them that other learning matters more—the math, the history, the literature.

This book will suggest that much of that talk is potentially damaging to the human process of learning and that we should be acting in opposite ways by encouraging those kids to use basketball as the starting point for significant intellectual growth.

This book will argue that by dignifying their love of basketball, by helping them turn it into a metaphor for the learning process, we can motivate these students to focus on the cognitive skills that matter. Student Choice Curriculum argues that if we can tap into the interest level of a young learner who wants to be better at basketball, we can use that motivational force to engender improvement in other academic and intellectual interests.

I want people who read this book (both teams) to appreciate the possibility that important cognitive gains can come to any person from an in-depth exploration into the things they already love. Basketball is something many young people love. Let them use it to frame their learning. I bet their gains will be tremendous.

I believe in public education, but I fear it is being treated poorly and that we may be nearing the end of its life as a positive force in American culture. This scares me, not because my livelihood will be affected—I'm nearly ready to retire—but because the good that public education can do will be lost to future generations. Education is a testament to potential, not only of the individual, but also of the community.

To diminish its central importance or to misrepresent its power through consumerist paradigms is to treat one of freedom's bedrock institutions improperly. I don't know that I can stop that, but if there is a way to engender a nationwide conversation about it, I'm willing to play a role.

So let's talk.

Chapter 1

Learning with a Purpose

Education is not something which the teacher does . . . it is a natural process which develops spontaneously in the human being.

—Montessori

FRAMING THOUGHTS

While exploring this chapter, consider how personal interest has played a role in your own intentional learning, perhaps asking yourself to what extent your schools might have capitalized on student interest to improve instruction. Moreover, you might wonder how prescribed, formal instruction possesses the potential to hinder significant learning. As this book hopes to promote conversations about educational reform that dignify student choice, you might ask yourself how your educational experience would have been different if you had been allowed to choose the topic of interest through which your high school education would have been framed. If one function of education is to help students live in the world, why shouldn't students be able to define their world and determine how they will be taught?

Think about the last time you learned something important. Perhaps it involved the raising of your child, or the training of your pet. Or maybe you learned a new technique for landing a fly in just the right spot of an eddy on a river, thereby giving you a better chance of catching the elusive rainbow trout when you travel to the Blackfoot River in Montana this summer.

Perhaps you're a golfer or a tennis player or a skier or a mountain biker so maybe your most recent lesson concerned the selection of equipment to enhance the enjoyment your hobby brings. Perhaps you're a musician or a photographer or chef, and your recent lesson dealt with emulating the methods of a well-known master, expanding your skill set into new creative opportunities for your art.

Or you're a heart surgeon or a massage therapist or a teacher or a firefighter who returned from a session at a national conference where new techniques were presented. Maybe you got to practice those techniques on simulators that showed their value. Lessons like this have immediate consequences, as they strive to create systems of better living, ways to improve your quality of life. Lots of possibilities come to mind when thinking about recent learning experiences, but most of them probably came from a deep personal interest in how the outcomes might affect your life. The learning would make you better, and being better is something you seek.

Not all learning is like this. Often humans learn things accidentally, through a life test placed before them. Many human tragedies come about because people fail these tests, then, perhaps, if they're lucky, they learn what they could have done to avoid a later disaster. So it is possible you identified a life lesson you had no plans to learn; they were not lessons you set out to learn from the beginning. This book won't be about those lessons, though it may offer some help for the times they rear their heads.

This book will be about the lessons people choose for themselves, the lessons that come from inner desires and pleasure centers. It will be about lessons that frame identity, the inner drive that recognizes knowing more means being more of what you wish to be. This book will be about lessons for which people open their minds and invite necessary enhancements to make their learning rich. There is an awareness that intentional lessons make up a good portion of our mental state. If you are reading this book, you probably believe learning to be a path toward a more controllable and better life. Choosing to learn enhances both learning and life experiences.

More to the point, this book will argue that choice will make institutional education more effective. Allowing high school students to choose what and how they want to study has the potential to connect them more directly to the learning process, thus it can help make them better learners. Current educational practices fall short of preparing young learners for the world ahead of them, mainly because schools place learners in situations that do little to motivate their learning skills. Allowing them to choose what and how they will study opens up opportunities for recognizing the same kind of experiences you recalled in the opening paragraph of this chapter.

This book recognizes that student choice is a new idea in American education, and that many forces presently work to deny it at almost every turn. If student choice were the ruling paradigm, there would be little room in our schools for standardized tests. If student choice ruled the day, there would be no textbook companies or software manufacturers dictating what books and tools our students would be able to access. The freedom student choice would bring to learners would make the systematic way we conduct education almost unrecognizable. And it would make it better.

Education speaks a language of choice today, offering "academies" of various topics and themes and providing students with an assortment of elective courses as they move through their four years of high school. Parents are encouraged to choose schools where their children will get the best education possible; performing arts and STEM schools are major parts of most educational districts. Choice is even being allowed within the context of the standardized testing movement as some families choose to "opt out" of particular tests.

But the truth is students are led down a very narrow path of options, and very little in our educational practices invites them to investigate their learning interests. They are rarely given opportunities to delve into what excites their minds. Thus, high schools graduate young people who neither understand nor have developed their own relationship with learning; who do not see a clear connection between life and learning; who have turned away from intentional learning as a method for solving their problems; but who readily utilize thumbspeak to find "answers" in electronic gadgets that do little to stimulate the learning processes of their minds.

This book hopes to spawn a conversation about how real choice could change American education. It hopes to get teachers and parents and legislators and even those in the ivory tower of higher education to talk about the only choice that really matters in learning: student choice.

THE GROSS CLINIC

A man standing among five other men gazes pensively off to his right. He is leaning on his left hand, which we don't see; in his right hand is a scalpel, held deftly by his bloody thumb and forefinger. The others around the table are differently engaged in the surgical opening of a human thigh. One, with fingers red like the man's, is probing a bloody chasm with a tool; both his hands are involved in the action, and his face is close to the opening, focused intently on his work.

A second, with bloodstains upon his sleeve, has another tool at the ready, handle toward the man. Looking across the action, he knows that the moment is near when an exchange of tools will be necessary.

A third looks down at what appears to be the towel-wrapped head of the person receiving the procedure. Is he consoling the patient? Is the towel drenched with anesthesia? That man's concentration sees only the patient's face. Is he avoiding the blood from the opening in the thigh? Is he allowing

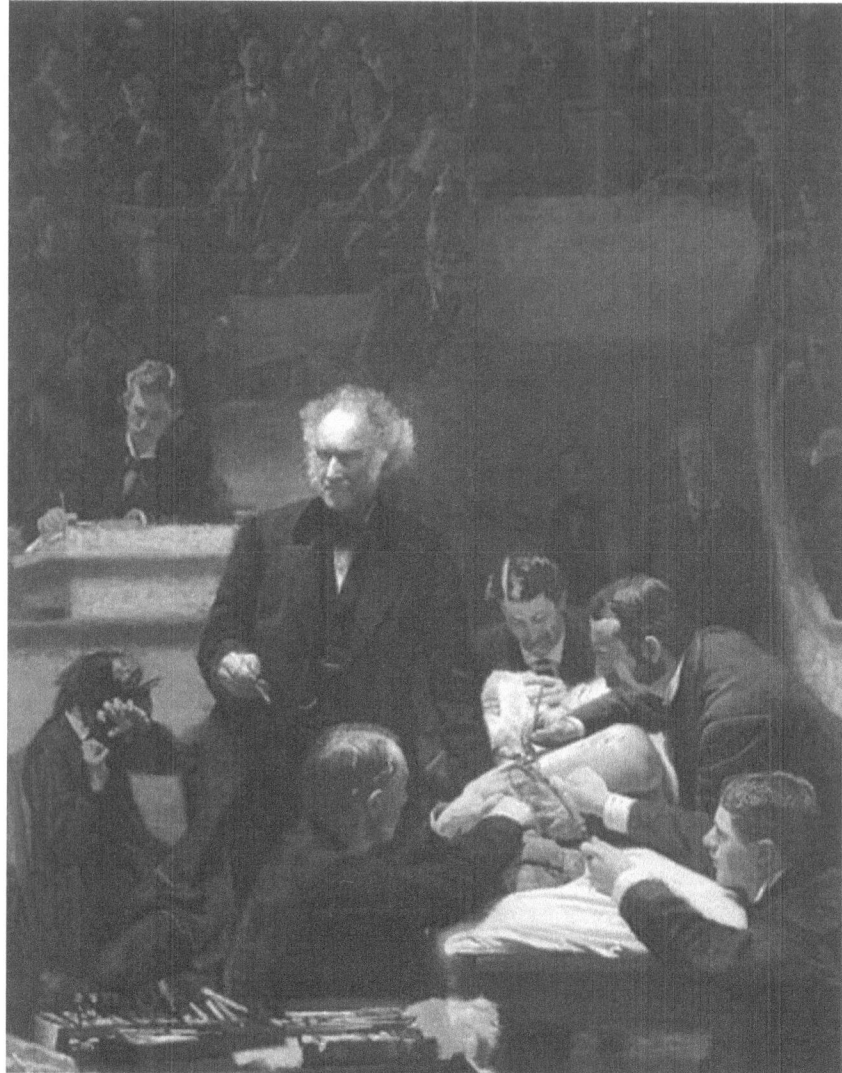

Figure 1.1. *The Gross Clinic*, by Thomas Eakins, 1875. *Source*: Philadelphia Museum of Art

only so much of his participation as he knows too much will be more than he can take?

A fourth reaches out, pointing toward the bloody chasm, perhaps noticing something missed or asking a question the standing man may answer. The fifth, down in the shadows, recoils at the ghastly sight of open, bleeding human flesh, obviously not ready for the task at hand. Why is he so close? What put him in this group of learners?

The man standing in the center is a teacher—a preceptor in medical jargon—and his task this day is the instruction and hands-on practice of a surgical procedure on a human limb. In the shadowy background a number of onlookers and students are engaged in typical student behavior. One is down front, sketching or writing in a notebook; several are watching intently from a distance; others have their chins on their hands, perhaps thinking, perhaps dozing, perhaps wishing they were down at the table sharing this perfect learning opportunity with their preceptor, or perhaps that they were in another class, or out about on the campus.

The portrait, *The Gross Clinic* by Thomas Eakins, dating from 1875, shows Samuel Gross, preceptor, ready to make an instructive comment about the procedure. Eakins has bathed him in light, drawing our attention to his forehead and graying, professorial hair. It is a stereotype, but only momentarily. Memories for teachers and classrooms like the one depicted here, of authentic action and intensive engagement, even if we are medical students, are hard to find.

In light of current accusations toward the American educational system, this lack of memories that evoke hands-on interactive learning is important. Moreover, it is not just the lack of memories that matters. Simply put, *The Gross Clinic* shows us that good learning has much to do with how a student approaches the learning at hand—is it of personal interest or is it for some other reason the learner is there?

Education for most has become a one-way process where the teacher has been charged with providing information to the student, and in most educational experiences that distribution has come through lecture or simple telling. Learning like *The Gross Clinic* depicts has been put in the closet of forgotten methods; students today are presented with information that prepares them for tests they must pass in order to prove to their local board or state or nation that they have mastered the material and may matriculate to the next level (or not).

Overall, the portrait offers an impressive starting point for discussing major challenges facing education—How do we teach the skills needed by twenty-first-century citizens? What are those skills? At what speed will the changing natures of those skills evolve? There are many more. The portrait, in depicting the art of interactive learning, probes the questions: What is learning? Where does learning occur? When does learning occur? How do we make learning happen? How do we make learners better (and how do we make better learners)? As well as the most overlooked question of all: While teaching occurs, who learns what and for what purpose?

Each of these questions should exist in the contested environment that is education today, but they do not. Rather, education has become an environment pushed and pulled by many interests, but not by a critical examination of methods, including the probing of significant questions.

Ironically, one of the significant interests that push and pull at education these days is choice, the idea that parents ought to be able to choose the school their children attend, no matter where, relatively speaking, they live in regards to that school. The idea has an equal amount of support and opposition. One side believes that the forces of the market, let loose by vouchers, will allow good schools to rise and prove their greatness while the bad ones sink to the dung heap of no return. The other side believes that voucher systems will destroy public education and limit the educational opportunities for the lion's share of our population.

Most families will not be able to send their children to the "best" schools, no matter how valuable the voucher, so some schools will gather the children of the well-off and well-educated, thereby perpetuating a kind of educational elite, while the other schools will lose resources based on full-time enrollment and become less and less able to give students what they need to obtain a semblance of the good life in the twenty-first century.

The picture is bleak because it is an image drawn from the wrong initial definitions of education and choice. If education were reimagined, repurposed based on the right definitions, the picture would change not only drastically, but quickly. That's the conversation this book hopes to help start.

CHOICE

Choice is understood as an ability to select from among options. It is a decision toward an alternative course of action. Most people find these circumstances positive. They believe that making decisions is better when options are plentiful. Americans have come to believe that choice is their due; its capitalist economic system does its best to provide choices in almost everything, from toothpaste to telephones and laptops to lavatories.

Choice even exists in the nation's mythic structure. Every student learns very early on that the Pilgrims came to the New World to choose for themselves how they would worship their God. Ever since, Americans have connected choice directly to the good life; we cringe when there are no better seats for the show, no better houses for our preapproved mortgage cap, no other models of minivan or SUV at the dealership. In recent years many have applauded the rise of Lyft or Uber or VRBO or Airbnb for having placed more options into the service industries used in vacation travels. Such options put more cities on the list of travel choices.

When seeking information about health, patients want a second opinion so that they can choose from different medical procedures and doctors. People like it that they can choose their president, governor, senators, and congresspeople, both nationally and statewide (even if turnout at American polling places is generally down compared to worldwide voting). Americans want to choose and they want to believe that they can and do make good choices.

Of course, counterarguments rebut this idea of plentiful choice, pointing out that choice does not always provide positive returns. Barry Swartz writes and speaks clearly of how too much choice can raise anxiety in consumers; that the overwhelming choices in today's markets bring about feelings of loneliness and depression. People are confused about what to buy to feed and clothe their family. What some see as a path to more freedom often causes a breakdown in the quality of life for both the individual and the community.

The idea of choice poses contentious issues for many people. The simple act of allowing individuals to choose which public restroom they could use exploded into a national debate in 2016. Marriage choice brought about a similar unease for a longer time, and the decision of the Supreme Court did little to quash the vitriol it raised. And forty-four years later, a woman's right to choose an abortion, the law of the land, still raises the hackles of too many people.

Choice is important to people; they fight for and against it; they apply it to nearly everything and seek it, for themselves, their families, and their communities. Some want the chance to choose the schools their children attend, extolling the belief that if a school is not performing up to par, it should be the parents' right to move their children from their neighborhood school to another school, a better school of their choice. They claim to believe that choice will help assure their children's success and future. They claim it as a right.

This book, in presenting the idea of Student Choice, will suggest that parental choice of that nature is a misguided goal, not because of the anxiety or depression that such a choice may bring, but because true educational choice should spring from the minds of the learners, not from the often misdirected dreams of their parents. Make no mistake: school choice should happen, but it should be given to the students in conjunction with their parents, not just to their parents. Choice should be informed by the student's interest, a mental place where she can see a practical reason for pursuing the explorations that learning entails.

Student Choice Curriculum is long overdue; it is the fodder for a great conversation. All other forms of choice, described by so many ideologues, have done little except diminish the nature and quality of America's public schools. Schools are experiencing significant drops in morale, as well as difficulties keeping credentialed classroom teachers. Moreover, students are becoming less connected to the process of learning, something necessary for making life better. That these phenomena are ongoing is obvious to anyone who has spent time in our classrooms. A significant misunderstanding of choice is dismantling an institution that has a reasonable chance to refocus American goals back toward life, liberty, and the pursuit of happiness.

EDUCATION

Education should not be a capitalistic process; it does not benefit from the whims or the supply and demand of the marketplace. Education is a community endeavor that draws students from the local environment to provide opportunities for exploration and intellectual growth, so they may dabble in the issues of the day, and develop a fondness for problem-solving that has personal practicality. At its best, education is both personal and communal, instilling a sense of place and value for community as well as the abstract constructive processes we call thinking and learning.

Citizens of progressive societies embrace the promise that active learning is the proper behavior when problems arise in their community, in the family, or in the individual's life. Citizens of conservative societies should do the same. This is not a partisan issue. Life mystifies all participants. Learning to function within the framework of those mysteries, to understand how to scaffold flexible and creative solutions, is necessary for success in any human experience imaginable. These are central tenets of education from which we seem to be retreating.

Education should serve students and communities simultaneously, seeing in both a connection of wills that pursues higher standards of life for all, as education is a significantly democratic process. Democracy functions poorly from a top-down formulation, but derives its greatness from grassroots populists who fight for individual and group rights. Strong democracies, the kind Rousseau advocates, are valuable because they get at the heart of freedom and human rights. All people come together to affect the contract under which they are being served. Anything less results in less freedom, fewer rights, and soft democracy.

Education is no different. Students are taught properly when they are able to name and frame the services they receive. Neither legislators nor bureaucrats, not even local school boards, should make the decisions about curriculum or evaluation methods; rather it must be students who determine and clarify goals and desires and then, in negotiation with their teachers, design the particular course of study they will follow—not by block or grade level, but as individuals.

Schools can maintain academic departments and a bevy of assessment strategies from which students can choose, similar to how democratic elections offer candidates and referenda that help frame the voters' minds. Moreover, schools can suggest particular learning processes and goals when choices are being made, similar to how candidates (but hopefully more honestly) present platforms and promised policy agendas while on the campaign trail.

Curricular scaffolding can be constructed so students continue to grow pertinent skills aligned with their choices, just as experts enter the political arena to offer interpretations and insights regarding issues that need a broader base of understanding for attaining right outcomes. Many choices are possible for changing the nature of America's educational paradigms, but the originating choice of the exploratory topic must come from the student, just as the decisions that make a robust democracy must come from the people.

In schools it is possible on a much more regular and intimate basis to query individual students about goals and desires and to shape learning opportunities based on individual determinants. The contact students have with their teachers; the input they share with their peers and other age-mates; their sought-after connection with the zeitgeist of the day, all give them insights into how they want to live and learn, a practice adults in our world equate with the very necessary freedom of choice.

To think of education otherwise is to liken it to the training of a domestic animal. While many claim the process is highly enriching, successful outcomes benefit the owner/trainer to a far greater degree than anything the animal experiences. In today's world of standardized testing and rigid curricula, schools reap the rewards of high grades when they successfully motivate their students to do well on the tests, while students often find themselves unable to navigate the world at large upon graduation.

Education should promote creative, critical, and flexible thought that has direct application to the learner's life; it should value the systems, biological and social, concrete and abstract, that make up what Fritjof Capra calls the web of life; and it should encourage the habits of mind that engender problem-solving and the more important problem-finding.

At its best, education spirals and loops back upon itself time and again so that the power and scope of learning are reiterated to both the learner and the teacher. It reshapes and repurposes informational processes. It is dialectical but never dictatorial. It listens more than it speaks. In other words, education must stop telling students what to learn and begin showing them how and why learning functions as it does, engendering in them the idea that when they know how to learn, they will have the basic steps for addressing problems that confront them.

STUDENT CHOICE CURRICULUM

Student Choice Curriculum will create that paradigm, allowing students to frame learning processes around sets of topics that already hold significant interest for them. All learners invest more cognitive energy into topics that raise their gooseflesh. Each of you recalls hobbies and passions upon which you spent mental and physical energies in the pursuit of greater excellence. You wanted to be a better tennis player or wine aficionado; you wanted to be a Civil War buff or to build your own backyard gazebo; you wanted to be healthier so you invested in yoga and not only found a local studio but also created a space at home for Hatha yoga.

The quality of an individual's education is contingent more upon what that learner brings to the learning environment than how that environment establishes a learning space, though both are important. Even the best teachers cannot, with assurance, bring learners to the Pierian Spring and imagine they will drink willingly. However, if those same learners have discovered their own thirst simultaneous to being shown the well, they will drink with a purpose that matters.

This component of education is greatly misunderstood. For too long educators have believed they could devise core curricula or standards that can be presented systematically to develop internalization and assimilation. Classroom experiences for the past two decades, perhaps all the way back to *A Nation at Risk*, show how the move to choreograph and standardize all that is to be taught has left fewer outlets for the creative students in public schools, and the accomplishments by which success is measured in those classrooms have lagged behind the rest of the world's.

Student Choice Curriculum will centralize the learner in a process of exploration of her own basic design. In that light, learning becomes more of a field experience and the learner a primary investigator. Teachers will be ever present to nudge and tweak the learner back into focus when the normal parts of adolescent life get in the way of focused learning, things like new significant others, experiments with social media that go afoul, must-see movies, illegal sleepovers, and so on. You know the drill.

But tweaking will also occur in more academic elements like the unfamiliarity of how to conduct a professional interview, the tentative nature of taking a stab at a new writing style, the lack of savvy in finding reliable research sources. These too will be fodder for teacher intervention.

For the most part, then, think of Student Choice Curriculum as student-centered learning, though understood as exploration more than explanation, where the teacher monitors the learning environment while the student navigates the contested spaces her own plans have brought to life.

Student Choice Curriculum will insert an element of fun back into school-based education. Fun may seem like a small thing initially, and many educators often pontificate how their lessons are designed for student learning, not for student enjoyment, as if the one can't include the other. But without fun, learning loses its value. Fun creates the willingness to transfer or to juxtapose so that learning moves smoothly into new environments, solving new types of problems.

Without fun, the learning stays in the classroom and never changes life's perspectives. Fun and play have been central elements to learning throughout recorded history, and their importance has been noted by exemplary teachers such as Plato, Jean-Jacques Rousseau, William McGuffey, Lev Vygotsky, Jean Piaget, Maria Montessori, and Richard Feynman. Each of these gifted teachers knew that learning is enhanced when learners are motivated by interest and enjoyment, and they did much to make sure their teaching included what made their learners happy in the learning process.

Another great educator, though not of the classroom, Mark Twain, was surely right when he had Tom Sawyer understand "that work consists of whatever a body is *obliged* to do, and that play consists of what ever a body is not obliged to do." And just like everyone else, Tom will take play over work anytime.

As the opening of this chapter suggested, the energy we muster to learn is correlated to levels of interest, along with goals and purposes—that is, fun. When you're exploring something compelling, you give it more cognitive space and allow it more actual time. The same must be true for the high school sophomore who, like Elvis Presley, carries his guitar to school every day, the junior who is perfecting her three-meter dives, the senior who is checking out the colleges of fewer than ten thousand students east of the Mississippi, and the freshman who, every day after school, talks with his English teacher about the best science fiction written in the past thirty years.

Each of these students has a passion that matters directly to their lives right now. Thus, each possesses an entry point for learning that holds great potential for rich exploration. Allowing these students to use those passions as frameworks for learning, allowing them choice within their educational process, enhances the nature of their commitment to the learning, helping them see that what they love is understood through learning concepts and cognitive disciplines that can be used in many other areas of their lives.

In other words, allowing them to choose their path of study will, in the hands of good teachers, allow them to grow their knowledge in history, science, math, and the humanities that matter to their community. Ultimately, it will also convince them that such a foundation of knowledge is a good thing for everyone.

This choice is worthy of a national conversation. Current educational systems clearly are not serving American communities in any way one would call democratic. The United States is experiencing more inequality of wealth and health than at any other time in history; a country created by immigrants is speaking—though, thankfully, not as one voice—as if immigration is the problem; a nation that speaks of freedom as its great gift to the world imprisons more people than any other country on the planet. These problems may not derive directly from poor education, but an inability to educate well influences the way all problems are solved, just as it influences the outcomes people face in many other social injustices.

Please note: Student Choice Curriculum is not a panacea to cure all ills. Schools cannot fix what a community cannot see or imagine. The argument here is that we need a transformative talk about how to provide a richer, more personal, and more transcendent educational experience for the young minds of our country. They need to learn how to explore deeply so that as they and their world continue to grow and to change, they have the proper tools to deal with that dynamism.

NEW SYSTEMS OF UNDERSTANDING

Because this is not a research project, the reader won't find detailed methods or particular measures of sampled groups who did or did not use choice within a set of parameters. While that approach may need to be used at some point, and while data are valuable components of critical understanding, many things involving education are better understood intuitively, not that which requires significance or validity as expressed through the jargon of social science and experimental protocols. Human beings have, across all cultural systems known to history, discovered learning to be a positive and natural practice that can make life better.

People grow when they are educated. They solve problems more effectively through steps that have been explored educationally, through behavioral repertoires that have proven their efficacy time and again. But it is also true that humanity had a long stretch of time where formal, institutional education did not exist, where parents taught children the lessons and beliefs of a tribal group.

This tradition of shared education occurred over a much longer stretch of human time than that which has included institutional education. Through countless millennia, humans learned quite well how to address their problems. If they hadn't, there would be no humans on earth today. So specific data are not necessary to know that effective learning derives from an individual learner's needs; history and common sense demonstrate that when learners put their particular needs to the intellectual challenge, learning happens.

Those who will argue data must come first—as some who read this will—should investigate Harry Harlow's monkey experiments of the 1950s. Harlow's central finding was that baby monkeys preferred to cling to stuffed animals rather than models made of uncoated wire. Indeed, his monkeys sacrificed necessities to cling to the furry rather than the wire surrogate. Go figure. Harlow could have asked any primate keeper at any zoo about his hypothesis—I was a keeper for nearly three years in Tampa, Florida—and all of them would have predicted his outcome exactly. To them such a finding was a no-brainer and a waste of research dollars.

The same is true with educational research. Most teachers know well what will and will not work in the classroom, without needing data or studies from academia—yes, I have worked in postsecondary education, too. Common-sense elements work in education, just as common sense can explain the behaviors of young primates. So while this book hopes to promote significant conversations about Student Choice Curriculum, it does so from the perspective of a common-sense understanding of education. Learning and education are complex undertakings, often requiring the creative application of thought experiments toward new ideas, which may then open up possibilities of more rigorous experimental work.

Richard Rorty calls this process "philosophical system-building," the "inventing [of] a new context on the spot, so to speak." System-building like this comes about because traditional experiments and meaning-making analyses have failed to uncover solutions that explain phenomena clearly. As often as not, Rorty claims, traditional experiments and meaning-making analyses fail to identify the right problems.

Many researchers come at education from a distance, misunderstanding the educational environment. Perhaps because they've left the K–12 classroom and moved to the level of professor at a research university; perhaps they were never much in the classroom in the first place. Or it may be that their "publish or perish" work environment forces them to see solutions from a numerical, data-driven, authoritative paradigm.

Educational reform must derive from a different direction, not from the top-down approach that all reform has seemed to incorporate. Rather, it should come from a more grassroots underpinning, beginning from the core of learning, not the elevated beliefs of too many learning theorists. Student Choice Curriculum will turn educational reform on its head by, figuratively speaking, putting the students in charge.

Top-down reform, as found in accountability and standardization movements, imagines education as a set of numbers, something by which we can see success and failure in data gathered from student tests. Reformers believe these practices reveal the quality of both a mind and a school, and that they can make changes in both that ameliorate educational problems. Thus testing protocols are mandated; higher, more rigorous graduation standards are required; and specific lessons about sundry topics, all with nicely scripted monologues for teachers to read to students before the learning begins, are inserted into the curriculum.

Is it any wonder that years of reform have not brought about significant, palpable change? Contemporary reform has tweaked the mechanics but not the humanity of education in search of solutions, believing that challenge and rigor make the mind function more effectively, whereas in truth it is not learning that creates the complexity of the mind but rather the complexity of the mind that creates learning.

Little has been done in the past forty years to improve the educational system, and when something does not work for that long, it is time to change plans. We must reject the idea that education can be delivered to the learner in neat little packages and reframe our approach with an emphasis on how the learner creates her own knowledge and understanding from interactions that derive from her own interests. This will democratize the educational system while simultaneously helping young people to see that learning is valuable and worth personal energy.

It has always been true that education should make people appreciate the power and the function of learning. Self-knowledge is increased when learning is done well, and democracy depends upon significant understanding of self in its citizenry. How else can justice and fairness emerge?

The United States has a long history of denying too many people the chance to be educated, robbing millions of the power and appreciation of self-understanding, deep and pertinent learning, and the potential to take charge of their own lives. Every day we do not openly and fully work to put that history behind us we fail our children, our country, and our planet.

Thus as Rorty's process of philosophical system-building allows education to be unpacked differently, Student Choice Curriculum stands as a possible paradigm shift through which the nature of the educated American can change. Students will learn with the purpose of expanding their own interest and understanding of theories and inclinations that matter to them. They will come away with a better understanding of the nature of learning, and have more control over the kind of lives they will choose to lead.

Student Choice Curriculum, first and foremost, will help students learn how to learn, in ways that already are a part of the human learning paradigm. It's that simple. And it starts by getting people to talk about it, for it is a conversation we truly need. Student Choice Curriculum is a positive way of educating, as it is cognizant of the individual learner's mind, letting her innate and personal complexities—call them nature and nurture if you wish—be the starting point of her academic explorations.

It's time to move in that direction.

DOUBLING DOWN ON THE MAJOR ISSUES

1. When learning is driven by need and interest, it plays a more significant role in the construction of a person's identity.
2. When learners actively engage with topics that feed their curiosities and passions, learning improves.
3. Good learning correlates with how energetically the student approaches the tasks.
4. Learning is enhanced when learners' personal interests frame the engagement.
5. Students should be allowed to choose curricular topics and evaluation methods within the educational program in which they are enrolled.
6. To serve learners more properly, education should shift from its top-down process to a bottom-up practice.
7. Education must stop being about facts, theories, and formulae and start being about method, function, and meaning.

Chapter 2

Linking Academics with Interest

If a child can't learn the way we teach, maybe we should teach the way they learn.

—Estrada

FRAMING THOUGHTS

All of us have been learners, and most of us have attended school for a major portion of our lives. Thus, each of us knows how our high school history or math classes worked and did not work while we were enrolled therein. Some of the questions, then, that should frame this chapter include a reflection on the processes that connected you to certain classes and teachers. Where were you allowed some sorts of choices, and how did those choices influence your interest and energy? During the time of high school, what were your real passions, and how might a focus on them have improved your participation and outcomes? Did you feel a part of your school and the study it promoted? Finally, the reader is asked to consider how education might actually limit the freedom of students involved in the process, pondering whether this is a positive process for our democracy.

Student Choice Curriculum allows students to select their focus of study from a nearly unlimited, mostly unwritten list of topics. Not many topics would be taboo. Depending on the local community, there may be some, but in the brainstorming context this book incorporates, the reader should imagine a near limitless set of choices, all based on the interest each individual student brings to the bargaining table.

Imagine students selecting from the following topic areas to frame their high school education: guitar, skateboarding, the American Civil War, computer programing, colonizing Mars, prehistoric cooking, marine biology, sound recording, Emily Dickinson, Harry Potter, pottery, backpacking, video games, Nietzsche, anime, eco-activism, lucid dreaming, fly-fishing, single-payer health care, finish carpentry, robotics, hospitality, sports medicine, auto mechanics, solar-powered flight, science fiction, scuba diving, and, of course, basketball. Those twenty-eight topics barely touch the total number that might be selected by a student body.

All offer rich potential for in-depth, interdisciplinary exploration over an extended period. More than likely, each represents a topic or pastime for which a student has already practiced or developed a passion. It is not too much of an imaginative stretch to believe a student can be quite involved in skateboarding, scuba diving, and video games—interests that motivate students to invest cognitive time in the learning process.

Once the topic is selected, the student networks with teachers to assemble a team of guides to assist in her exploration. In this light, Student Choice Curriculum becomes a socially constructed learning environment, incorporating the interests and skills of multiple stakeholders to take advantage of the social nature of both schools and the human species. Students and teachers—and students and students, and teachers and teachers—will create a learning journey that will help the student develop the physical and mental expertise necessary not only for intellectual growth, but also for interacting successfully in a complex society.

In this chapter, the reader will see how basketball serves as the topic of interest for a bright young athlete, Lindsey, a ninth grader at her Student Choice Curriculum high school. Lindsey and a team of teachers will effectively assemble a learning plan through a focused study of basketball. Student Choice Curriculum uses active learning theories to focus attention on the innate interest students and teachers bring to the educational landscape. It is democratic in that no one person oversees the entire process; rather different leaders will emerge at different times in a shared, holistic understanding of what education could be.

A CONDUIT OF THOUGHT

Student Choice Curriculum works from a premise that valuable learning of any topic includes the learning of critical, evaluative thought. Such processes, once learned, can be transferred. When a student "loves" history, or when she says she's "good" at history, she ought to be communicating her comprehension of how a historian works with data, prioritizes information, and constructs historic theories and narratives. She should be looking forward to navigating the field of historic thought from within a framework of primary, secondary, and tertiary sources, so she understands how different theories of history change the way those sources might be interpreted.

In other words, she is not only saying she likes things "back in the day," but also that she involves herself with the interpretation of human life as it has been reported by historians who have researched (and appreciate) things back in the day. She should be able to observe how different times and places have seen history differently, in part because interpretations of history change over time, but also because of an awareness of the myth that history is told only by the winners. She will understand that history is written and understood in the present, and that should give her a better understanding of how the human mind works no matter what the scope.

A student who loves history should be learning the hows and the whys of historical thought, making her mind able to construct historic knowledge on its own or in collaboration with others of similar ilk. Sadly, that is not how history is taught in our high schools—or math, science, literature, or any of the subjects high school students take. And, of course, for most students it would be very difficult to accomplish this task in high school as most high schoolers will not come to history or math or science or literature with that kind of knowledgeable drive.

But they will come to learning with that drive for deep and transferable critical thought if they are allowed to explore something for which they already have a deep passion. If given the chance to take significant steps into the understanding of basketball, its history, its science, its math, Lindsey will be motivated to develop deeper understanding of how those practitioners work in the world of knowledge. She will enjoy the process because it will center on what she already loves.

This is not to say that a graduate of Student Choice Curriculum is ready to be a historian, or mathematician, or any of the viable careers that arise from intense study. Rather it suggests that digging deeply into significant aspects of academia, framed through personal interest, provides a sense of how to improve quality of life. She will know if she wants to dig in deeper and to do the very specific work of collegiate study in her chosen subject area, because she will have had several conversations with her teachers and several members of an authentic audience about just such an option.

Thus, Lindsey will have a good idea if she needs to change areas and investigate another path of academic interest, and Student Choice Curriculum will allow her to make an easier transition to another field of study because she will have learned about knowing and practicing and producing knowledge inside a topic area. Such information is surely transferable, and such transferability will be one of the ways Student Choice Curriculum measures success.

Schools don't do that now; we don't ask students to learn about the ways scientists or historians or mathematicians think or work in their fields.

History is not taught as a discipline that creates and evaluates knowledge but rather as a collection of facts and information of that discipline. There is a significant difference. The same is true of every course taught to high school students today. Students are not asked to think within the field; they are asked only to know some of the facts the field explores.

That last thought may beget murmurs of dissent from teachers in many high schools. Teachers of all subjects often believe the standards they have created engender mental development well beyond rote memorization of simple facts and information. That may even be the case in their particular school or classroom. But most students report, even the gifted ones, that classroom work is about covering the factual material, that which will be tested, from start to finish, be it contemporary world history or British literature or algebra.

If you ever challenge those students to demonstrate newly gained classroom knowledge, their modus operandi will be to share sets of simple, often quite misconstrued facts and methods; they'll insist that World War I was started by the assassination of Archduke Ferdinand, that Columbus discovered the world was round, and that William Shakespeare didn't write the plays that carry his name. Rarely will you hear them put their learning into a personal, internalized theory of utility; rarely will they transfer what they've learned to ponder or predict a current social dilemma.

Yet ask one of those students about her interest in, say, fly-fishing and she'll talk about her roll or curve cast; she'll tell you when and why she would use a wet fly; and she would even be able to tell you why she might use a wet fly in a dry-fly context, in words and details that would show you she knew her stuff. In other words, for the things she has a developed interest, her internalized understanding is rich, broad, and flexible.

That's the kind of learning that should be sought from our students, learning that serves as an entry point into the very important world of problem-finding. Current educational paradigms do not value or create anything near the personal ownership that will lead to thinking that leads to problem-finding. Indeed, it is rare to find solid evidence that schools encourage students to solve real problems. Student Choice Curriculum could help reverse that status quo and develop a system where students internalize skills that engender both problem-finding and problem-solving.

Student Choice Curriculum understands disciplinary practitioners as knowledge creators; it develops students who investigate how knowledge is approached and created within their chosen topic area, speculating that students will use their personal interest to internalize both the processes and the products of that knowledge. A basketball player like Lindsey has within her the love and appreciation of the game that will serve as a conduit to help her understand productive cognitive skills.

These skills and attitudes will allow her to see that when she confronts the strategies of an odd-point half-court trap, she is using the mental skills that will let her understand the strategies of a business or housing or busing decision made by a local or regional or national political party. Her interest is a path to make her wiser.

CHANGING THE TERRAIN OF LEARNING

When history is understood as a discipline that creates knowledge, the student must see herself as an explorer into methods practitioners use to create historic understanding, to be a historian. When that occurs, a different set of experiences fill the learning environment. Different questions are asked; different activities are practiced; different assessments measure the work. The terrain of learning changes. Classroom engagement will not focus on methods students already have internalized, nor will it explore things for which students already have answers.

With Student Choice Curriculum, the goal is for students to explore areas and processes they have only previously imagined doing and have, perhaps, set as significant goals for later learning. Moreover, a clever and creative teacher will lead students toward information and methods they did not necessarily know could be connected to their topic of interest, thus expanding learning potentials.

At the end of the process, a different kind of student may emerge.

Rather than possessing a collection of facts and information, this student will have the skills to discover problems, specific tensions that help advance a field. To be a knower within a discipline you must be a problem-finder. Yes, facts and information matter, but within Student Choice Curriculum paradigms knowers are challenged to understand the nature of their field of interest and the kinds of problems it seeks to uncover and solve.

Current paradigms seek something very different, something simpler, something less motivating. Unfortunately, schools have received what they sought. Students learn material, take tests, and write papers, and then generally forget what they have learned. This forgetfulness should not be surprising. When learning occurs outside of a contextual framework, it is harder to internalize, for it is context that makes learning matter. What is taught doesn't help students solve problems, because it doesn't come from a place students see as real or applicable to their own lives, from a place they might have found themselves.

In the real world of disciplinary knowledge where real practitioners do the work of history and math and science, problems drive the learning. A problem prompts practitioners into action; they hypothesize what would happen if, and they conduct experiments and engagements and hypothetical applications to understand how to deal with the problem. Student Choice Curriculum approaches learning that way, so many more students will be able to appreciate and apply specific disciplinary learning upon finishing the program.

This chapter seeks to show how Lindsey and her teachers can effectively navigate the terrain of building skills in both mental and physical modalities, while allowing Lindsey to explore basketball across the curriculum. To see how this works, two central questions need to be asked:

1. Can basketball serve as a vehicle for the kind of independent learning that will lead a young mind toward personal problem-finding and problem-solving?
2. Can we use an interest in basketball to guide a learner through the intellectual demands of history, science, literature, and mathematics, so she becomes a knowledgeable practitioner of those fields?

The answers are overwhelmingly yes.

HISTORY IN STUDENT CHOICE CURRICULUM

By choosing basketball, Lindsey has selected a sport somewhat unique to the United States. It is played almost everywhere now, though modern basketball begins with James Naismith in Springfield, Massachusetts, in 1891. But, Lindsey will discover, some historians suggest that something very much like the game was played hundreds of years earlier in Mesoamerica, and a chronology of multicultural events can be explored here.

Moreover, basketball has an internal chronology that has resulted in many changes to the game and to the rules as known. All basketball fans seem to know about the peach baskets Dr. Naismith hung from the overhead track, and how the ball had to be punched back out of the top of the basket when a shot was made, but there are other elements that students could explore in order to understand the historic progression of the game, including (but not limited to):

- It didn't begin as a five-on-five competition.
- Specific game actions like dribbling, fouls, and the movement of the players have often gone through significant changes.
- The dimensions of the court changed over time, as did the layout of lines of demarcation on the floor.
- There was once, in many places, net "caging" around most courts, giving the players the once very popular nickname "cagers."
- The nature of the ball has changed greatly over time.

Some of these changes seem to have popped up inadvertently, while others represent particular eras and purposeful intention within the game's growth and development. Understanding these historically would help a learner explore how historical knowledge and theories are constructed and how such constructions offer frameworks for investigations into other historic issues. In other words, Lindsey would be asked to look at significant methods of historic thought and knowledge development in her understanding of the game she loves so to be able to transfer those methods and developments to other aspects of historic thought.

Moreover, as with all good histories, there are opportunities to make inferences and value judgments about quality and development, similar to how historians of wars or social movements talk about strategies or events as moments of significant change and influence in particular historic contexts.

Rule changes along the way have both helped and hurt basketball, depending who you ask. The shot clock that began in the National Basketball Association (NBA) was incorporated into the collegiate game several years later. Purists still question the collegiate adoption, citing media pressure rather than quality-of-play issues as the deciding factor. Coaches spoke out about the collegiate shot clock, with Bobby Knight positing that if real change were desired, the time of possession ought to be fifteen seconds, not twenty-four or thirty. Thus, there is a full history to explore therein.

Regarding media's effects on changes in the game, certainly the fact that basketball games are nearly ubiquitous on television from November to June, show that influence. This influence brought the "TV time-out," something that initially occurred only in televised games but now appears in all collegiate games. Obviously, no games prior to television were affected by this rule. Allowing Lindsey to investigate the nature of these rule changes and to defend or reject them by merit will help her understand how a historian works in the field, testing hypotheses and seeking consensus. Such investigations are a great way for a student to engender skills in critical thought and historiography.

It is important to note that deep thinking need not only be about the highbrow topics we associate with academics. Certainly it is worthwhile if students learn to communicate clearly in speech and writing about the causes of the American Civil War, women's suffrage, and the New Deal; and certainly the thought processes that can be developed through such engagement are necessary for a growing set of critical skills. But to imagine that similar skill development cannot be had about basketball's history misses a major point.

Critical thought is a cognitive process where the knower measures and juxtaposes facts and inferences which bring to light insights and action plans for future outcomes. That which happened has a set of sources to be considered, and the phenomena have ramifications toward some significant principle. It could be health care, the wealth gap, censorship and the First Amendment, or any issue you can imagine: significant critical thought can be learned by a deep focus on any of these ideas. In Student Choice Curriculum, the belief is that a topic like basketball allows the same deep focus and, thus, the same critical, cognitive development.

From a historic context, basketball can be seen and understood through theories that formulate significant historic perspectives. In this light, Lindsey could consider changes to the game, including, say, the stature of the arenas where it is played and the money made by the players, owners, and leagues through a Marxist lens. Perhaps she could look at the same issues through Hegel's Dialectic. Both of these perspectives are used in the teaching of Global Politics and History of the Americas, and students find them to be compelling ways to think about history. There is no reason why such paradigms could not be brought to basketball's history.

Clearly basketball has become big business, and any historical understanding must include both a social and economic focus. As the world becomes more global in economic practice and political interactions, students need to be able to understand the rich world of socioeconomic theories. Student Choice Curriculum allows this understanding and complexity to be approached through an exploration of something the student has a passion for—in Lindsey's case, basketball.

AN INTERLUDE

Let's open this idea of history a bit wider. The reader is seeing how basketball has the potential to meet the demands of a significant concentration in history, and that nothing would be lost within a study of history if Lindsey were allowed to use basketball as her focal interest.

But there's another element in basketball (and nearly all other potential topics) that makes Student Choice Curriculum a better way of guiding high school learning: By selecting basketball, Lindsey opens up the potential to mine the people of her community for stories and patterns of the game's local history. Players from long ago had an impact on a population of fans, leaving legacies of seasons and games and styles of play that still resonate in the hearts and minds of many.

It is not hard to imagine that a daughter or son is following in the footsteps of a parent who was a local star, something that creates a historic study in itself. Contemporary schools have built new gymnasiums or, maybe, new arenas, and such changes have influenced the history of the game in that locale. Maybe the fans were closer to the floor in the old gym, making the experience of playing or watching much different, or maybe something idiosyncratic about the old gym caused fans or players to behave differently while there.

Allowing students to choose their topic of study will, in part, force them to investigate the people of their community who know the history of their choice. It will allow them to "do" history. The curriculum will still be dependent on the learner/learner interactions, and the student will need to be encouraged to step further into that academic area that is history so as to make that local flavor come alive. But it makes sense that Lindsey will enjoy engaging with former basketball players, coaches, and fans as they tell her the stories of how things were "back in the day." Such engagement is the stuff of education.

HISTORY IN STUDENT CHOICE CURRICULUM

Of course, we shouldn't forget Santayana's adage (untrue though it may be) that those who do not know their history are condemned to repeat it. Thus Lindsey could explore those moments in basketball's history that seem to repeat themselves: the mistakes players, coaches, and leagues have made time and again even as better minds might have done otherwise. This is a lesson in interpretation that will force Lindsey to make value judgments regarding how major decisions are made within a context. History is up for interpretation; even the interpretations of great historians are fair game.

Such is the same in basketball. Great teams have not won the championships many thought were their due; leagues begun with fanfare and financial support suffered, shriveled up, and died; players thought of as the next greatest player proved to be only adequate and not able to meet the demands of the competition at the next level. How do such beliefs crumble? How do dynasties die? Basketball holds a key to understanding history so long as the student and her teachers engage with the interest and then design a proper exploratory plan for the study.

Moreover, when Lindsey focuses her exploration through basketball, her experience of the game can become a metaphor for many other learned phenomena. For example, if she understands the way the game is played in the most common of settings, the driveway, where neighborhood kids come together to play pickup and H-O-R-S-E and twenty-one and myriad other games, she can understand how the "rules of the game" create social cohesion.

If you've ever played driveway basketball, you know how local rules take over. They have to. In driveway ball, the hoop may be nailed to the garage, often with a piece of plywood serving as backboard. Thus the garage wall is often contacted in any aggressive play under the hoop. Would it be out of bounds if a player touched the garage while in possession of the ball or would it be okay to touch the wall if forced *into* it by an opposing player? A local rule would determine that. It thus becomes a cultural difference. Such differences are important components of a global historic understanding.

In different driveways, the game of basketball is always recognizable: an observer sees jump shots and rebounding, passing and dribbling, fouls and violations, but in any given neighborhood, players amend rules to their own acceptable preference. Different neighborhoods allow different players to call fouls; different check-rules apply after a basket; different clearing rules dictate play after a rebound or a steal. Learning those local rules is significant, for, without that knowledge, a player could not join in that driveway game.

Thus, basketball becomes a metaphor of learning, allowing juxtaposition, assimilation, transference, and creative problem-solving. Moreover, it forces the learner to see nuance and subtle variations in the applications of knowledge gleaned. When local playing spaces change, say to a cousin's driveway in an adjoining town or to the full court at the park, where kids from many neighborhoods gather to play, the player (or learner) understands she must bring all that she knows of the game so that once on the court, she can move smoothly into the flow of this particular game. She knows the rules will be slightly different and that the players will emphasize different elements of the game, but if she's done her work, she'll find the proper entry point and be an asset to any pickup team looking for a player.

A challenging assignment would be to get Lindsey to juxtapose several different sets of driveway traditions in her own town, compare those to the different levels of play in that town—full court at the park, half court at the recreation center—and then to compare those structures with the way several different towns in her state structure their local government. Metaphors matter to growing knowledge.

Thinking of basketball metaphorically lets us recognize that every neighborhood with a basketball tradition has its own socially constructed knowledge of the game, which, of course, makes that neighborhood and the game itself no different from the social world in which all people live, where day-to-day existence includes having to learn many things that emerged from socially constructed traditions.

With basketball as a metaphor of learning, Lindsey will be able to transfer her understanding of the game and its rules and the local rule-bending to the larger scale of social and political organizations, and thus explore how cohesion in those contexts also often breaks itself into social groups of vastly different practices, just as the players of differing neighborhoods do.

This is no small matter in a world where diversity is a growing trend. Understanding differences between, say, Chicago Democrats, national Democrats in general, and democrats with a small "d" is central to understanding governmental organizations and social systems within the United States. Each faction plays by rules particular to its own geography, but each also knows how the rules diversify when an individual crosses over from one level to another. A recently elected Democratic mayor of Chicago knows that both particular and general practices will have to be altered if she wants to become a national player in the Democratic Party.

Understanding the way modern societies ebb and flow within and around each other is essential to being a good citizen in those societies. Often those local politicians have to make the right decisions quickly if they are to develop the kind of reputations that will allow them to play on a national level. They need an inner sense of political acumen, a clear understanding of the rules of the game.

Good basketball players need the same mental skill. They come to know the game well enough to leave behind their own neighborhood rules when they change locations of play. Often within one or two possessions of the ball they find a way to fit in. If they don't, they won't get picked for next game, and maybe won't be welcomed back to that neighborhood anytime soon.

The basketball and social elements just alluded to await the clever construction of learning goals by the teachers and the students. With the latter focused on the game, the former can do the initial creative work in the academics, forging connections that may seem new at first to the learner. But through negotiation, and through time, those connections will coalesce into more internalized apprehension of the way life naturally unites through lived experiences.

A central paradigm within Student Choice Curriculum is that the predetermined order of subject area curricula is up for debate within each individual's learning program. In other words, requirements that a study of history begins with American, world, or European surveys do not exist; explorations won't be divided geographically or chronologically. Rather, teachers will be charged with finding a fit for the topic of interest within the subject area so that students will be challenged to grow necessary and general skills in history, math, science, and so on.

Schools have long relied on these preset plans of matriculation, and quite frankly, they have not been effective. American students—high school and college age—are notoriously bad at finding Zanzibar on a world map; they don't seem to know the governmental processes we generally teach as "Civics"; and they rarely can name their city, county, state, or national representatives. While facts and dates do not describe the goals of history or geography education, when students are unable to put particular and general historic facts together, they are also quite unlikely to think historically with any skill.

When this skill is lacking in any subject area, students find themselves unable to navigate critical problems that regularly occur in their lives. As I write this text, the University of Florida is preparing for a campus address by white supremacist Richard Spencer, who prefers to be labeled a white nationalist. Most of my students have little awareness of the event, of the fact that Florida's state government is spending nearly $500,000 in added security for this one event, or of how Spencer's presence brings to light basic problems the United States has with issues of liberty, freedom, and justice.

One of education's chief functions must be to show students how to live in the world. To do this through the inherent interests of the learner makes good sense. Young preschool children play with each other and mimic what they see in the adults around them. They play in this way because they see that these particular and general behaviors are what people do, and they, the children, are interested in becoming people. High school students are no different. Their eyes and ears are attuned to the world around them, and they would, if they could, mimic the behaviors of the people they want to be.

Lev Vygotsky and Jean Piaget are adamant advocates of enriching childhood learning with play. Interest is a natural way of encouraging the learning process, a natural way of developing educated people, those who make decisions that move their societies toward sought-after ways of life. When people understand better, they make better decisions. Using personal interests in the learning environment allows each learner to see into the metaphors that shape human understanding more clearly.

All human phenomena deal with social dynamics, and thus even basketball can become the metaphorical framework for seeing life more clearly.

NEGOTIATING HISTORY AS CURRICULUM

One of the goals of this book is to frame a significant conversation on the potentials of this Student Choice Curriculum. No significant change comes without the natural ebb and flow of critical conversation among practitioners. To probe that a bit, focus your mind on the very beginning of high school, when Lindsey has made up her mind to make basketball her focus for those learning years.

To make her decision, Lindsey must meet with several teachers in order to find entry points and personal mentors for the subjects she'll apply to her study. She'll speak with a couple of history teachers to find out who would be the best fit with basketball; she speaks with some math and science and English teachers to do the same.

Once she has a list of names, she'll engage those teachers on the skill set she sees as directional, and she'll listen to the teachers who will guide her in accomplishing that set. They will, surely, add to her package of expectations, reflecting on what was mentioned previously: Lindsey will not be saddled to the normal order of classes in any subject area but rather will be directed toward the kind of thinking in that subject area that fits her choice.

This selection and recruitment process will be guided and aided by several assemblies, several "open houses" by each academic department, and lots of posters around the school directing, encouraging, and generally orienting students to the process of creating their own course of study.

Most of the organization of these three weeks could be handled by students, many of whom will be third-year students and focused on their own study of event planning or recreation counseling, two topics that might get many students interested these days. Even if no such interest is selected at a school, there are always ways to motivate students to help organize school-wide events, so these first three weeks will be in good hands.

Requirements will dictate that a student *cannot* enroll in Student Choice Curriculum without having met with teachers in all subject areas; indeed, at least two teachers in each area will need to be part of each student's plan. This initial orientation will need to be completed by the end of week three.

To facilitate scheduling, each student vying for a Student Choice Curriculum position will be required to meet with perspective guidance counselors in that third week, solidifying all plans and recording all decisions. As it may happen, Lindsey may discover that her meeting in guidance is scheduled for Monday of week three, so she will need to have most of her information in order earlier than other students.

This will be hectic; it will be difficult for many of the students to navigate this world. So it will be necessary for staff and students to be ready and willing to help where help is needed. Thus, schools using the Student Choice Curriculum will need to be smaller, perhaps schools within a school, so that cohorts can be established and students will know the others who are in the same boat.

Still, anyone who has worked with high school students knows it doesn't take long for most to figure out new systems or to find friends who will help, even if the student is quite shy. They find each other; they work together. With a helpful staff and student body at the ready, encouragement and direction can go a long way to make this orientation run smoothly.

STUDENT AND TEACHER ENGAGEMENTS

As Lindsey informs her teachers she wants to make basketball her study, it is fair to imagine that one or two of them in the department will not know the game well enough to be helpful. In truth, it is possible that an academic department at a high school may not be able to find a teacher with a passion or even a good clue about each student's interest. If so, Lindsey will need to know that she may continue her goal of studying basketball but without the guidance of a staffer who really gets the game.

That should be okay: history is a discipline, and as such has a core of significant theoretical approaches, all of which might be used to understand the game. The history teachers would know of these approaches.

Of course, basketball has a chronology—all professional sports do. Even one who has never seen a game understands that the game comes from somewhere, it has a history, and is populated by individuals who have experienced that history from multiple perspectives.

Thus, good guiding questions from inside the discipline of history ought to be discernable by a high school teacher, who can, through negotiated conversation, direct an interested learner toward an appreciation of the skill set of this field of study. So even without the wherewithal of the game, one or two teachers could be found to lead our young learner through the maze of connecting history to basketball in an academic structure.

But let's imagine Lindsey finds two staffers who know the game and are excited to work with her. One of them will almost surely want her to explore the aspects of race within basketball, challenging Lindsey to discover how the game dealt with racial issues, and how those events shadowed or illuminated similar growth or progress in the United States.

Sometimes, that teacher may note, when the country made racial progress or experienced backslides, the game followed suit; sometimes when the game made racial progress or experienced backslides, the country followed suit. Great moments of racial tension and release run through the history of sports, just as they run through the nation's history. Part of Lindsey's study of history will surely be an exploration therein, with papers to write and presentations to deliver that allow her thinking to be shaped and evaluated.

Her other teacher might want to investigate the nature of the game's introduction and rise in American culture. This fairly traditional approach is often less stimulating for students. But given that this teacher is also a hoops fan, she can engage Lindsey in a discussion of the game's origins, finding out just what she knows about Naismith, Springfield, and even the Mesoamerican game that bears some similarities. "We're going to learn about the historic markers and the comparative elements of the game in such a way that you'll know more about how history works," she tells Lindsey. "One can't really know about a game without having some sense of where it started, and why."

In fact, it might be decided—and here the two teachers should confer on their own availability as well as the coherency of the study—that Lindsey will take on this historical perspective in her first year, and leave the racial elements of the history for her second year and beyond. Race is a deeper issue, with more critical connections to the fabric of America than just the history of the game. Teachers will make assessments of Lindsey's skill set and place these two units of study in context. (A partial outline of Lindsey's study appears at the end of chapter 3.)

In Lindsey's second year she will again meet with teachers and fine-tune her program. She will know that she accomplished her history objectives in her first year (or that she did not) and needs to move forward or revisit some of that work. She seeks out the teacher who recommended the racial angle, reminding her of last year's idea. They agree to pursue this task, then talk about the first African Americans to enter the NBA, with Lindsey mentioning that "Sweetwater" Clifton, Earl Lloyd, and Chuck Cooper each hold a distinction in opening the racial barrier. It is something she read when she studied the history of the game last year. So they chat about Clifton being the first to sign an NBA contract, Lloyd being the first to play in an NBA game, and Cooper being the first to be drafted by an NBA team.

Lindsey, who has matured, indicates her goals to conduct some in-depth investigation on the continued role each played in the inclusion of African Americans as well as how they are seen and regarded by a league now so fully integrated that white players are clearly in the minority. Moreover, she wants to juxtapose how two other professional leagues—baseball and football—opened up their racial barriers, with regard to the same entry points as the NBA: contract, draft, and first playing experience.

The teacher recognizes Lindsey's personal commitment to this project, especially how her personal interest and previous year's study motivated it, and tells her to create a unit of study, including potential assessments, and to get back to her by the end of September (Lindsey's school begins on the first Tuesday after Labor Day).

With that challenge in place, Lindsey spends some time thinking through many of the projects and presentations she completed last year and imagines a unit. Then she arranges to meet with her teacher on September 28. Prior to the face-to-face, Lindsey emailed a rough outline of ideas and products, chronologies and potential resources to her teacher, revealing that she, Lindsey, is becoming a little knowledgeable on the nature of a learning plan.

Lindsey is thinking of creating a significant PowerPoint slideshow, a formal 1,600-word paper, and the creation of a true-false test she hopes to give to a bunch of volunteers—locals and schoolmates who call themselves basketball fans—to see how much they actually know about the game's racial history. She's got some books, and she knows some locals who have been a part of the basketball scene for many years. She's considering a six-week time frame for the work as it will fit well between now and the scheduled vacation at Thanksgiving.

She and her teacher talk:

Teacher: Hey, Linds, tell me about your PowerPoint slideshow.

Lindsey: I wanted to bring together a bunch of photos and weave in some text and audio of old-time announcers, of how the racial makeup of the NBA changed the game tremendously, but that it took more time than many imagined.

Teacher: What are your resources?

Lindsey: My dad has a big collection of books about old-time NBA players and coaches, people like Bill Russell and Red Auerbach. He also has a book about the Harlem Globetrotters. I've been looking at a bunch of those for years, and I'm pretty sure I can get almost all of what I want from them.

Teacher: Good, I'm glad you're thinking about print resources. But I'm sure you know that there would be a lot about that on some pretty significant websites, like the Naismith Memorial Hall of Fame and the NBA site.

Lindsey: I know, but you've been on my case (she grins) about using actual books, and Dad has all of those, so I figured this would be a good time.

Teacher: Yeah, well, that's my job. You also should know that Coach Rankin, our athletic director, has a very good mind about the game and has been connected to some pretty big names around here and nationally. You should really try to spend some time with him. (Pause while Lindsey writes notes.) Who's your audience for this PowerPoint?

Lindsey: I'm not fully sure, but I thought Mr. Jacobs (history teacher) ought to be a part of it since he loves hoops and knows his history. And I want to get both boys' and girls' basketball teams to be there.

Teacher: That works for me, Linds. And I can tease up some others. How big a presentation will this be?

Lindsey: I'm not sure. I've already got a bunch of information, so I think it might take me ten minutes to deliver it by the time I'm done with maybe thirty slides.

Teacher: That should be fine. And I like the date, but I want you to meet with me here (she points to a date on the calendar) at the halfway mark so I can check your progress. You'll bring the slideshow, well, as much as you have done at that point, and your learning log to that meeting.

Lindsey: Right. (She writes in her notebook and looks back up.) I figured I'll give you the paper on the day right before we go on vacation.

Teacher: I don't think so. I'm going to want that the Friday before so I can read and evaluate it before you go on vacation. Then, if it is not up to snuff, I'll assign a rewrite for the vacation. (Lindsey looks concerned at this potential, and they look at each other intently for a long minute.) The way I see it, Lindsey, I'm going to let you tackle this paper on your own. We won't meet in the middle and discuss progress as we have with your other papers. You're becoming a good *writer, so I need to give you space. You'll write what you feel is necessary, fill up the 1,600 words—don't go over—and give it to me here* (she points at the calendar). *I think this will keep you more honest about the work. If it's good, no work over vacation; if it's not, I'll want to see a significant revision on the first day back after Thanksgiving.*

Lindsey: Okay. (She hesitates, obviously not liking how that went.)

Teacher: *Look, there has to come a time in this process when you do the work you're capable of just because you want to do good work. I can meet with you time and again and redirect or reteach certain elements, but that can only work up to a point. A Buddhist concept holds that "the final job of the teacher is to free the student of the teacher," and we start that final job with the first job. I'll look over your PowerPoint, especially as that will be an authentic audience assessment. But since I'm the one who'll read this paper, I want you to write it for you, but with me in mind. You've heard what I've had to say about your writing up to now, so do what you know I want.*

Lindsey: *I get it. I'm just not liking the possibility of writing a revision over the break.* (She writes a few more notes.) *The true and false test?*

Teacher: *I really like that idea, but I'm wondering, what do you intend to do with the results?*

Lindsey: *I don't know. I just thought I'd score the tests and find out how much the kids did or didn't know.*

Teacher: *Why not weave the ideas of your PowerPoint into this true-and-false test?*

Lindsey: *How do you mean?*

Teacher: *Well, Lindsey, you tell me; what do you think?*

Lindsey: *Well, I guess I could take the results and figure a way to give the kids the information they didn't have. Maybe in a handout or something.* (She was struggling and didn't really see where her teacher was headed.)

Teacher: *Yeah, maybe. What else?*

Lindsey: *Uhm, I guess I could give the true-and-false test first instead of after and adjust the PowerPoint based on the results.*

Teacher: *Yeah, perhaps. But I'm thinking that maybe those kids could become part of your audience for the PowerPoint show. You're thinking about fans for the true-and-false test, but you only mentioned players and Mr. Jacobs for the PowerPoint. Now I know that the players are surely fans, but I think you can scratch up some fans who don't play for our teams, don't even play much ball themselves, but still like the game. Then maybe you could make a prediction of scores—keeping in mind that guessing can work well on a true-and-false test—and all who score below must attend your PowerPoint presentation. That could* *increase your audience, and when you're done, you can lead a discussion with everyone there. The opportunity to share will be tremendous, and you then get another chance to work on your own speaking skills in real time, something we still need to see some major improvements on.*

Lindsey: *I don't know. That's more than I had planned on.*

Teacher: *I figured that. So I'll sweeten the pot. This now becomes an eight-week unit, and you can test and give the PowerPoint after Thanksgiving break, taking this up to Christmas break.*

Lindsey: (Liking the sound of that.) *Okay. I think I see what you mean. So does that change this* (she points to the date for the midway PowerPoint meeting)?

Teacher: *No, I don't think so. We've added some significance to what you're going after, and so I still want to know that you've got some good stuff planned at that point. If this all works well, my suspicion is that even if your paper is great, and you don't have to work on it during break, you'll want to keep working on your PowerPoint slideshow and make it tremendous.*

Other similarly negotiated conversations will occur often in each subject area during the year.

CARRYING IT OUT TO AN END

Thinking about this differently, Lindsey's teacher may focus this racial issue as a major thrust of the study and not just a six-week unit. Negotiations will be different, and Lindsey may be asked to do a lot of writing early on, developing a racial exploration in her first year when her work is more tightly focused on factual data and the differentiation of primary and secondary sources, as well as the contextual basis of cultural forces upon the game.

Then, in her second year she could move her understanding to a level where she can publically present internalized information, filtered through a Hegelian or Marxist paradigm to a mixed and authentic audience of basketball fans and players.

By her third year of study, two developments may occur. It is possible her teachers feel comfortable she has met the requirements of history for formal graduation. Her work may be that which allows each of them to say "congratulations, you've completed this part of the Student Choice Curriculum requirements." Two years of history is often an adequate demonstration for many high school districts in America—and if it's not, it should be, if done properly. Or maybe she'll be asked to do a bit more work, mainly because her teachers are not quite sure that she's demonstrated the depth of skill to call her work complete.

Here the teachers may suggest particular readings or products or performances, perhaps like the creation of high-quality videos on the nature of race and racism in basketball and to share these with journalists and video production people within the local area. Everything here would remain grounded in an exploration of how historians construct knowledge from theories and how they use theories to evaluate knowledge.

They might also have her revisit a particular work from year two so as to revise it into a better product. As with the earlier teacher-student dialogue, these would be negotiated spaces, shared discussions of why the teachers need more work and how they want the student to process it.

In Student Choice Curriculum, one key is that with all Lindsey's learning, she and the teachers work together to create not only the nature and range of the exploration but also the manner and weight of assessment. As history is very much a subject learners interact with verbally—students read the histories which tell the stories of the created human world—then language will be very much a part of her assessments.

There are myriad ways to construct long-range plans for a high school student who loves her topic. Moreover, the current world of digital technology is full of possible resources at the click of a mouse. Things that could not have been accessed a couple of generations back are not only readily available to our students, but also very familiar to them, though it may be true that Lindsey has not yet thought of using YouTube to explore the racial history of the NBA. Resources only make themselves available when minds are ready to go to work. Student Choice Curriculum is ready and waiting to get that ball bouncing.

IN THE MATHEMATICS DEPARTMENT

Is the same true for mathematics? You bet, and with a ready ease.

Math experts everywhere claim that American students lack number sense, a numerical approach that develops a feel for what numbers mean, creatively and flexibly. They suggest that American students have limited mathematical cognitive abilities. Basketball could address this lack immediately as—just like all other sports—it intentionally keeps statistical analyses and applies them to every part of the game.

Significant statistical formulae are continually applied to every aspect of the game, so number sense will be activated. Averages matter in determining the quality of players and teams; all leagues—even fantasy leagues—use them to monitor progress and establish hierarchies. When Lindsey is computing and juxtaposing averages and statistics for the players she is exploring, a continued repetition of the numbers reporting points per game (PPG), shots per game (SPG), and minutes per game (MPG) will allow her to determine the effectiveness and value of a particular player or team.

Over time, working with these numbers, she will get an understanding of how data work, and she will look at different sets of data about random players and make sensible determinations about those players' qualities. If Player A averages more MPG but fewer PPG than Player B, an assumption of A being less effective is reasonable. If Player B also records fewer SPG than Player A, the answer probably becomes that Player B needs more playing time. She scores more points in fewer minutes, taking fewer shots. That is a kind of number sense, a mathematical process used by basketball people.

By selecting basketball as her topic of study, Lindsey can expect to develop a keen understanding of averages, mode, median, and mean, including the many ways each is used to illuminate differences in data sets. Along with that understanding, she will learn to converse intelligently about processes different statisticians use with data as they tell stories of the game. As she branches out to other statistics that apply to other elements of the game, she will continue to hone her number sense and become flexible in its use.

During this process, a creative teacher will monitor this work and challenge Lindsey in order to raise the ceiling of academic expectations. Such challenges will meet with Lindsey's acceptance in ways that similarly raised expectations to students are not, mainly because Lindsey will have an interest in the basketball numbers she is exploring.

For example, when her teacher gives her the names Pete Maravich, Willis Reed, and Kevin Garnett and asks her to determine if they would win a three-on-three game against Wilt Chamberlain, Chris Paul, and Tim Duncan, with the caveat that she can only use numerical (objective) and not narrative (subjective) data, the cross referencing and insightful flexibility of number sense will be shown quite well.

While many might see this as an unanswerable challenge—who knows what player will get hot and when—it will be how Lindsey supports her claim with the numbers, how she uses the data to tell the story and the outcome of the game, that demonstrate the skills her math teachers need to see.

Such a challenge evokes in the learner an understanding that numbers in themselves can tell a story, maybe not always the full story, but certainly a part of it. In other words, through basketball averages, Lindsey will understand what Disraeli meant about "lies, damned lies, and statistics." While she is exploring these statistical data, a creative and clever teacher will present her with similar tables that portray data from different disciplines to see what can be made of them, checking on Lindsey's abilities in transferring knowledge.

If the teacher gives Lindsey data concerning: (1) the wealth gap in America; (2) the carbon parts per million in our atmosphere over time; or

(3) the efficacy of health-care expenditures across nations, Lindsey ought to be able to make some reasonable determinations about those numbers through what she has learned through her study of basketball statistics, allowing her to approach the complexities of some major social ills.

For the purists, more advanced mathematics, like algebraic formulae can be brought into the mix with queries like:

> *If Dave Bing scored half as many points in the next three games as he did in the last six, and his average points per game was 23.5 for all nine of those games (the first nine of the season), how many points will he score in those next three games?*

Surely this is artificial—no basketball person would ever think like this in real terms. What Bing will score in the next three games has much to do with the previous six, but it also matters which teams he's playing against, whether they are home or away games, and other sundry elements.

But what similar algebraic equation is less artificial? When you think about it, who truly cares that (or when) two cars leaving two cities headed in opposite directions at different miles per hour will pass each other? Nobody. Such a problem doesn't matter in your life, though the reasoning developed for solving the problem may, indirectly. Thus, a clever and creative math teacher, using Lindsey's love of basketball to imagine new ways to write word problems, can create a link between that interest and mathematical thinking that "pure math" explores.

If we shift to a study of geometry, it is clear to see that a basketball court is made of large rectangles, small circles, curved lines—arcs—hash marks and other significantly demarked areas. Some of those marks indicate front- and mid-court sections; some divide the court into back and front courts; some establish the value of a shot made; some create a space inside of which an offensive player cannot stay for more than three seconds unless she has the ball and is moving toward the basket.

And the major lines of circumference divide in-bounds from out-of-bounds. Professional courts are generally larger than college courts; college courts are generally larger than high school courts. (However, at all three levels variance occurs, sometime for a purpose. Can you say home-court advantage?)

Basketball hoops are a specific size and so is the ball; a women's ball is smaller than a men's ball. The three-point line is at a different distance from the basket at different levels of play. The hoop is the same height across leagues, though this was not true historically: youth leagues, for a long time, used lower baskets, one of those decisions many in the game question as it can affect developing skills.

All of these geometric spaces can be measured, bisected, expanded, contracted, compared, named, and understood. Lindsey can measure adjacent angles, areas, and circumferences; she can explore the golden ratio or the sectors of a circle. On the ball she can see how Euclid's law of triangles comes apart through different applications of elliptical and Riemannian geometry. She could even figure out just how much paint is needed to paint a designer court, including the mascot, for her high school. An entire course of geometry can be taught through the designs on a basketball court.

Players come in all sizes too, and if she considers things like arm span of the five players currently playing defense, she can imagine how a zone trap at the mid-court line can function well or poorly depending on how long a span the total team has. Couple that with their quickness—how fast each moves across the spaces in that zone—and you're back to asking this algebraic query:

How far will player A need to move to assist player B to trap Opponent C at the mid-court line if her arm span is five feet ten inches and she's playing the point of an odd-front zone on a standard-sized high school gym?

As with her study of history, the negotiation between the student and teachers will determine the order these math skills will be addressed as well as how assessment protocols will be followed. Everything about Student Choice Curriculum is a negotiated space of learning.

Certainly Lindsey should expect that all mathematics will be tested in some common pencil-and-paper ways, and that plenty of opportunities to make oral presentations using mathematical data will be given. After all, one thing an expert on basketball might do for a career is become an analyst or play-by-play announcer.

But there are other ways to bring about a clear demonstration of the student's mathematical skills, and when the negotiation is inclusive, both the student and a creative teacher will think of them. For example, Lindsey could be assigned to create her own fantasy league of three or four teams, and then monitor their progress over the season. Within that framework she could be asked:

- To control team scoring averages by rotating her lineup, game by game
- To control wins and losses by selecting which players will play in which games
- To control all data points on one team, seeking outcomes that were superior to another, but with that team having a worse win-loss record

Each of these, and many more challenges could show how deeply Lindsey had internalized her mathematical skills through an activity she probably would be using anyway. She'd have to make real-time decisions based on the mathematics, and because she'd want her team to win, she'd do this on a regular basis, without prompting. If you've ever had a fantasy team, you know the spirit of competition can be contagious. Through such an assignment, her teachers would not only know if Lindsey was competent in math, but also that she understood a significant way to see into the fabric of the game.

Math experts report that students do better when they visualize numbers in arrays or patterns like a flowchart, something like metaphorical thought. Such practices are beneficial for developing sound and practical number sense. Yet most math classes use charts and graphs of sterile statistics that cannot motivate all students, if they even motivate one. Often these charts and graphs are of made up of data, or very old examples, generated to "teach a point," not to make a connection with the learner. Instructional paradigms like this fail to engender mobile knowledge as students don't take this classroom work into their real lives.

With Student Choice Curriculum, an interest in basketball will also let Lindsey consider how statistics are used beyond the world of basketball. Collected data from her fantasy league would allow ample opportunities for her to make predictions or provide analysis about the hypothetical season to come. Moreover, she could see how other data, like those from the wealth gap, global climate change, and health care, mentioned earlier, create opportunity for similar future-oriented predictions.

Good teachers could challenge her to find new ways to display numbers more informatively, emphasizing how numbers help determine decisions and outcomes in the real world of basketball and beyond.

Brain scans inform that mathematical facts are manipulated in working memory, and that this part of the brain shuts down easily when stressed or not well motivated. The interest Student Choice Curriculum capitalizes upon will fight this shut down by keeping Lindsey focused on information she already is motivated to explore. It is harder to be stressed when you're exploring what you love. Or, in other words, that which you love allows stress to be constructive, something that provides reasons to learn deeply.

The game of basketball supplies both contemporary and historic data, and there will be hordes of opportunities to mine those data for comparative information. Such availability provides myriad ways to assess the developing skill set in the student. Intuition and logic come together to help Lindsey frame foundational thoughts about the power of numbers. Moreover, these same numbers can be used to explore and expand the imaginative powers of her mind.

As has been suggested here, she can be challenged to select any number of fantasy NBA teams so that by the end of the season their basic statistics can be compared. All year long Lindsey will watch outcomes and make comparisons between teams, trading and playing different players to change success levels. She may have to change strategies to alter certain outcomes, even have to lose a game now and then to keep her statistics right. She'll probably love every minute of it.

So in both mathematics and history, Student Choice Curriculum offers clear educational access to learning and evaluation. The student's choice does not eliminate opportunities for learners to pursue traditional subject areas; it enhances those explorations. Considering the breadth of interest in our multicultural society, many students who heretofore have felt left out of the educational system will find a more significant entry point by being allowed to choose their own path of learning.

BROADENING THE SCOPE

Student choice can occur with every high school subject, though it seems unreasonable to detail each fully. If what has been said about mathematics and history rings true, readers should be able to bring ideas to the conversation that are pertinent from your particular experiences at your particular schools. However, in fairness to the other classes, a brief look at English, science, and the arts seems to be in order.

Without doubt, Lindsey's study of English can be easily shaped by the choice of basketball. A broad assortment of books is readily available, and not just on players in the zeitgeist. Coaches like John Wooden, Red Auerbach, Bobby Knight, Phil Jackson, and Dean Smith have written often and well about the nature of winning, of competition, and of human-resource management of all kinds.

Award-winning journalists have shared insights on the highs and lows of the game, covering not just the play-by-play but also the in-depth investigative journalism that probes players, seasons, and the human elements therein. Book-length works about Connie Hawkins or the exploits of the Fab Five at the University of Michigan tell important stories of how players can get hoodwinked along the way to stardom.

Some great writers have focused on basketball: John McPhee wrote wonderfully about Bill Bradley's relationship to the game; John Updike centered his Rabbit novels on a high school star; and Pat Conroy's *My Losing Season* is a thoughtful, poignant memoir. Lesser-known authors have provided exquisite narratives by focusing on the game and its players, creating connections between the big time and backyard ball. Pete Anselm's *The City*

Game is considered by many to be fairly labeled literature. An internet search of novels about basketball brings up myriad titles that focus on the game and ancillary elements regarding players and their relationships. It is a tournament of reading material.

Of course, English is not just reading, and it is not too difficult to see how a plethora of writing exercises and assignments can be created around Lindsey's interest. If Lindsey plans to make her living through basketball, we must recognize the unlikelihood of that being a player. As good as any player may be, chances of playing professionally are miniscule.

However, nearly every newspaper has a sports department, nearly every team has a publicist, nearly every city has several television channels that need local sports broadcasters, and there is really no limit to what a strong writer with a good mind for a story can do as a freelance writer. If the negotiations about assessment probe deeply into how Lindsey wants to approach the game in her near and distant future, loads of different writing assignments can be created with different readers as assessors.

Moreover, though in all classes she should be assessed in oral, real-time presentations, in her English class this kind of presentation fits perfectly: English is the home of oral presentation. Lindsey's teachers will want to hone her communication skills and assign her to arrange a series of interviews with former players or coaches. She'll learn to develop the skill of questioning and following up in real-time. Interviews will be transcribed, so a full set of writing skills will be developed.

Some interviews benefit from being turned into narratives or feature pieces that don't rely so much on the Q and A format but rather weave a tale in a particular context, so another full set of writing skills is used. Such an assortment of work could result in something a local paper might pick up, and within this framework she would be learning how to sell or submit material to actual print publications.

Basketball is a game that also lends itself to many kinds of scientific studies. Being a physical game, it can be bought to physics quite easily. Most people don't know that to assure a ball is of legal inflation you drop it from approximately six feet of height. If it bounces back up to just above four feet, the ball is fine. There's a formula for that—a scientific formula. Jumping, passing, running, setting a pick, blocking a shot; all these are physical tasks that can be measured empirically so that part of physics can be brought to the learner.

Basketball is called a noncontact sport, but force plays a very significant role in the game. Certainly the physics of endurance training, of weight training, of running, of aerobics, and of yoga can become part of the study.

But a more personal science could be brought to Lindsey's study, a science rarely taught in high schools, but one very significant for students in

America: nutrition. What does a player eat on game night? Why? How much? What do these carbohydrates do for the energy of the body? Moreover, a full exploration into claims of healthy foods and the science behind them—made clear by Michael Pollan's works—would allow Lindsey to evaluate how science works (and doesn't). And it might show her why nearly two-thirds of all Americans are obese.

Finally, it makes perfect sense that basketball could lend itself to a very significant investigation in the arts. It is a visual game: five players are moving all the time, with a big ball and little gear to hide human expression. Photography, pencil sketch, and video mosaic are wonderful ways to reveal what it means to be human. Long-range investigations of complex themes or short-range projects of individual works await only the negotiation of student and teacher. Art tells many stories, and sometimes the subtleties and nuances of real tension are made clearer through images than through narratives or expository writing.

Consequently, Lindsey's look into basketball's racial issues might find a perfect medium in the arts.

BEGIN THE CONVERSATION

The point is clear: as basketball could be a strong topic around which to design high school curriculum, so would nearly any other topic. Student Choice Curriculum reframes the learning process so that valuable requirements can still be addressed, but in ways that place the students' interest front and center. Interest and knowledge are intricately connected, and each begets the other to some degree. Most people want to know more about what interests them, and most humans become interested in the things they know and use in practical, personal ways.

A student who is allowed to choose basketball as her core topic of study will bring energized interest to the intellectual investment she makes. She'll lead herself to pertinent knowledge in other subject areas that connect to the game. As she learns more things about the game—how to break even-front zone traps, how the rules have evolved over time, and how the legendary Bill Russell felt about getting his number retired by the Boston Celtics—her new knowledge will spawn interest in other aspects of the game and broaden her study.

It makes sense that a young mind allowed to invest intellectual time into that which brings enjoyment will find intellectual investment to be of more value. Knowledge built from an investigation of a personal interest will be more easily transferable and more easily applied to issues beyond the topic area.

Student Choice Curriculum has opportunities to help young learners gain skills more traditional daily lessons do not foster. Interest is a great motivator when it comes to learning, something people know intuitively and through personal experience. Interest increases intrinsic motivation. Those of you who have taken on new interests have found yourself investing both time and money in your work to become better at them.

Perhaps you have developed an interest in golf and now find yourself reading articles or subscribing to magazines so you can improve your long irons or your short game. You probably couple this with occasional lessons from the local club's pro, and you find yourself spending more time than usual with YouTube golf tutorials, club in hand, in your living room. All this comes from choosing to learn because of your personal pursuit of digging deeper into a new interest. It is a basic process of learning.

Our students should be encouraged to do this daily.

Student Choice Curriculum has the potential to tap into Lindsey's passion in ways that she could dabble in the real-world practices of her interest. When done well, Student Choice Curriculum will bring teachers and students together in ways that our more formal curriculum does not. If Lindsey is hoping to work as a professional announcer or analyst for some media outlet, her ability to speak and think well in real time will be a necessary focus for all classes. Occasional negotiation sessions between her and all teachers would be able to chart a path that would have significant planned repetition and spiraling experiences of skill building.

No longer would a student wonder why it is that the work she does in English has nothing to do with the work she is doing in history, even though both seem to be focused on the time of the American Civil War. With Student Choice Curriculum, the teachers would be regularly working with the student to craft the network of interconnected activities in learning.

DOUBLING DOWN ON THE MAJOR ISSUES

1. Student Choice Curriculum is a socially constructed learning environment, where multiple stakeholders negotiate both the range of exploration and the scope of evaluation within the student's educational process.
2. Student Choice Curriculum takes advantage of both the social nature of humanity and the social network that is a school.
3. Learning is, and should always be understood as, a negotiated space.
4. The artificial order of topics and subject areas used today should give way to negotiation between student and teacher.
5. Any topic of interest treated with intellectual intent allows deep focus, critical thought, cognitive development, and transfer.

6. Learning, within Student Choice Curriculum, becomes an entry point to the skill of problem-finding.
7. When selected topics are seen as metaphors for learning, the ability to transfer knowledge is enhanced.
8. Student Choice Curriculum puts student interest front and center, thus deeper intellectual investment from students will emerge.
9. Learning challenges within Student Choice Curriculum will be met with more open attitudes, mainly because those challenges derive from the student's design of curricula.

Chapter 3

Student Choice within the Curriculum

A teacher's purpose is not to create students in his own image, but to develop students who can create their own image.

—Unknown

FRAMING THOUGHTS

What makes a good student? What makes a good teacher? All of us have probably pondered those two questions at some point in our lives, as we have been or are students, and some of us are or have been teachers. Consequently, these questions should be front and center on your mind as you engage with this chapter. Education must matter to you, or you wouldn't be reading this book. As the argument grows, keep your mind focused on your own understanding of how education might be improved by promoting student interest. Imagine how a high school might be differently organized to make the qualities of individual interest drive the learning processes of the students therein. How will teachers change? How might communities play a role? What might have been the transformative element that would have allowed you to make choices within your own institutional learning?

Public schools are populated by all sorts of students, teachers, administrators, maintenance workers, counselors, cafeteria staff, media specialists, and sundry workers from all walks of life. That should not stop. That demographic is essential to the qualities schools provide for the communities or our nation, let alone for its learners. At their best, human endeavors expand human potential. The more we expand and empower the creative spirit high-quality education engenders, by allowing all people to explore and construct their own understanding of liberty, justice, and fairness, the more we increase the quality of everyone's life.

Thus, when considering who will take part in Student Choice Curriculum, the simplest answer is any and all students who so desire. Still, to create the kind of conversations necessary to the critical evaluation needed for Student Choice Curriculum, it will be important for the reader to see a few of the students and teachers of this program. This chapter will bring some of those stakeholders to light.

THE LEARNERS

Lindsey

Lindsey is a high school freshman who loves basketball. She's been playing her whole life, in her driveway, at the parks, at the local gyms, for her Amateur Athletic Union (AAU) team, and she was a significant force on her middle school team. In part, she gets her love of the game from her family as both her mom and dad played high school ball, though not at the same school. Her mom played a little in college, the local state college, though she chose not to continue to play after her sophomore year.

Lindsey is a tall freshman, and the varsity coach is interested to see how she'll adjust to the high school game. Initial plans are to put her on varsity, but the coach has not ruled out letting her play junior varsity ball in order to get her more playing time. The local ballplayers know her, and when pickup games happen at the park, she's an early pick even when the games are coed. Nobody right now expects her to be a strong Division 1 prospect, but every fan who follows the local game knows she's one to watch.

One trait her parents have instilled in Lindsey is a good work ethic, and she knows how to pursue her game skills with dedication. She can spend an hour or more with the ball at the park and never take a jump shot; she can spend another hour or more and only shoot from inside the paint from a back to the basket starting position. She is aware that her dedication is unique. But she also knows—thanks, Mom and Dad!—that if she wants to make basketball her life, it will not be as a player but in some other capacity. She's seen the numbers, and she knows some of the kids who let false hopes leave them unprepared for what they didn't see coming.

Lindsey comes to Student Choice Curriculum with a sense of purpose that is focused on the many ways one can have a life in basketball beyond playing. In her head are prospects of being a coach, a scout, a journalist, a broadcaster, and any type of data-crunchers. She is also thinking that being a physical therapist for a team—college or professional—might be a good way to earn a living. She wants basketball to be her life, but she hasn't settled on a specific role.

Outside her love of basketball, Lindsey is a good reader and an adequate student in math and science. She has a natural propensity for languages, and she loves to use her camera. She isn't a natural writer, but she hasn't found that to be a setback at this point in her education. Call her a good kid all the way around, and that's the right scouting report.

These details are important because they are the entry points that allow Lindsey to appreciate the work she'll need to do to be successful in Student Choice Curriculum. Moreover, they are attributes her teachers will need to discern in their interactions with her, for, as with so many talented high school kids, Lindsey will hide them until they become noticed as her work and skill level grows. An immediate difference is that within a Student Choice Curriculum framework, teachers are challenged to find and feed the learning skills already present in the students.

This is not something current educational paradigms explore. Thus our schools only rarely know what motivates students to be learners.

Student Choice Curriculum excites Lindsey as she sees it as a chance to attend school and remain focused on something she loves. She believes most of her academics will focus on journalist elements of basketball at first—learning to write better, to conduct effective interviews, and to manipulate data into meaningful information—as that is her first choice for a long-range professional career.

She and her parents feel good about the idea that everything she does in the classroom will be connected to basketball in some way. They believe this will be a motivating force for her, keeping her focused on the development of many diverse skills. And they like the idea that Student Choice Curriculum puts purpose into the classes Lindsey will take in ways that purpose doesn't normally exist in schools.

Both parents are college graduates, but both know they went to college without clear plans about life. It was the logical next step after graduating from high school. One thing her father worries about is that by letting Lindsey study basketball there may be no "leverage" if things begin to go south in her schoolwork. In middle school they could threaten to keep her off the basketball team, though obviously if she's studying basketball, that punishment may not be valid.

Still, her parents know, and Lindsey has an inkling, that this is going to work well because the focus is connected directly to her interest. One last thing: Lindsey knows her older sister would never have been successful in Student Choice Curriculum, as she didn't have the self-starting mechanism for academics. Thus, Lindsey knows it might just be possible that she, too, will find difficulties and may need to be moved into the standard curriculum before her high school years finish. She does not want to let that happen.

Anthony

While most of this book will focus its examples through Lindsey, it is important to think of other students so the reader can frame different perspectives of how Student Choice Curriculum functions. Good teachers teach to the students in their classes; they don't design lessons for some prototypical kid. So imagining many kids here may serve our conversations more fully.

Anthony finds himself at the end of his second year, still a bit unsure of which interest he might explore as his main choice. In the ninth grade, he was an avid video game player who often met on Saturdays with friends at his or their houses for binge tournaments that could last all evening and long into the morning—much to his parents' discontent. He was good at games, and his friends knew him to be very competitive.

He found excitement in both single-player and team games, but his favorite was one-on-one, just him and one other player. He understood that games were not what his parents wanted him to do, and being one to follow their wishes, he never quite convinced himself that games could be a topic of study in Student Choice Curriculum. But if you were an omnipresent observer during Anthony's first year of high school, you would have understood him to be a gamer beyond anything else.

His parents both attended college, but neither graduated. His father found work with a local construction company and has become one of their site managers, an important job that fits with his high sense of organization. Anthony's mother is the office manager at a health clinic, overseeing a plethora of paperwork. They are a one-child family, and the three are very close.

Anthony's social network is not large, made up of other gamers roughly his age, but it does include some nongamers who, unlike Anthony, were involved in Student Choice Curriculum. Even a few of the friends Anthony binged with on weekends were enrolled. So Anthony does get occasional prodding from buddies; his teachers, too, try to interest Anthony in the program. But by the end of the three-week orientation session in his first year, Anthony had not found a way to create a topic of study, so he attended regular high school classes in the first marking period.

Something changed around the ninth or tenth week of school. Anthony became interested in how some friends were in his classes but occasionally not there. When he discovered how they were shaping their own world of academic adventure, Anthony took a more formal interest. Thinking back,

Anthony is unsure how he didn't get everything started for Student Choice Curriculum. It wasn't for lack of interests. Aside from gaming, Anthony enjoyed and participated in other activities that would have played well in a Student Choice setting.

Mostly it was that he couldn't understand how something he did for fun might be something he could do for academic growth. That divergence didn't connect for him. Many students will be like Anthony: they won't have the academic or imaginative background to wrap their heads around the program's goals. Had he talked with more teachers, sharing his interests more completely, he may have found an entry point earlier. But he didn't, and because the teachers did not know him in those first few weeks, there was little that could be done to bring him along.

But as the first grading period neared the end, Anthony began to speak with his teachers about joining Student Choice Curriculum. With some friends as support, Anthony shared his fear that selecting one interest would force others onto the back burner, and he's not ready for that. He shared his love of games, and a few teachers, especially his English and math teachers (the latter being a gamer herself) encouraged him to make video games his focus of interest.

There were many ways to make this work, they told him, and a couple of friends affirmed their encouragement as they, too, were using video games for their study. A little planning, a little cajoling, and Anthony became involved in Student Choice Curriculum by the second week of the second grading period in his first year of high school.

Then something happens to Anthony near the end of the second grading period, and he recognizes that his academic interest is changing. This will not be uncommon to any high school teacher, and it will need to be something for which every Student Choice Curriculum school must prepare: high school students change their minds often. Part of Anthony's change has to do with his interest in games: he loves to play, to compete, to live the experience of playing.

His teachers, though, want him to explore the nature of the story of the game (English teacher) or the way a game projects particular character types in the different roles of the story (psychology teacher) or even the programming challenges of the games he plays (science and math teachers). These intrigue him a bit, but not like playing. And so, on a near daily basis, Anthony feels that he ought to be doing more, but he cannot muster the energy to follow the guidance of his teachers, and the elements of Student Choice Curriculum are taking a backseat to his singular interest of playing the game.

Thus, by the time the school transitions to the third grading period—the last of the year—Anthony is shifted back into the traditional classroom schedule as he has completed very few products or plans that would demonstrate the criteria he and his teachers had set for his learning agenda.

The year ends, and Anthony is not feeling too good about it.

In the summer between his first and second year Anthony was learning to play the guitar, and signed up for subscriptions to several YouTube channels for tutorials. His parents liked this interest, mainly because he did most of this practicing alone, at home, and they both love music. His commitment amazes them, as it is not uncommon for Anthony to play for nearly five hours a day, several days a week. He still games some, and Saturday there are still tournaments at the house, but now Anthony plays his guitar when not involved in a game, and occasionally he'll even sit out a turn to practice a finger pattern a bit longer.

Anthony's parents like that their son is learning to play some of those classic rock songs they grew up with. Like so many parents, they overstate Anthony's ability with the guitar, but he can simulate many introductions or lead breaks from classic rock standards. Those few times they convince him to put on a show for their friends, he rarely fails to please. Some of his friends at school were recruiting him to be a part of a band, and by the end of his sophomore year, he will be ready to join them.

In conversation with his parents, Anthony expresses discouragement about not remaining in Student Choice Curriculum, and they agree to help get him restarted. All three go to the school a week before summer ends, and through conferences with administrators and guidance counselors, a plan is created and Anthony begins his sophomore year studying guitar as a performance instrument.

This works well for nearly the whole year, as Anthony studies the math of music; the history of the instrument and musical styles; the science of sound waves and communication systems; and the literature of music and artistic craft. He can write about music; he can read about music; he can study the sound made by music; and he can explore the influence music had on different cultures. He loves it.

But Anthony is like many high school kids. By the time the third grading period is in progress, his interest in the guitar is waning, and his teachers see it. They work with him to regain his focus, but it is difficult. A major parent-teacher-student conference is held where this team of stakeholders explores Anthony's work and interest as a student so that they may find a way to keep him in the program. If they cannot, there is little to expect other than two more years of high school in traditional classes. If they can, Anthony may find himself immersed in another personal interest when the third year begins.

In situations like this, Anthony's previous teachers must be consulted, along with his parents, as they have been privy to his developing skills in math, reading, writing, science, and history. Moreover, they and Anthony have experienced the various ways Anthony has expressed his academic interests.

With him very much involved in the conversations, they can discern a new direction for the working interest or an entirely new interest. They can encourage and recommend the amount of time needed to complete the academic plan based on how Anthony has demonstrated the skills he needs for graduation. And they can place the proper limits and parameters onto Anthony's program so he knows what he's accepting by staying in the program.

Anthony's situation will be a difficult aspect of Student Choice Curriculum. Students must be allowed to direct their own learning when they have a particular interest in mind. But the schools must redirect the student when needed. Options are always open to return to the normal high school schedule, but in Student Choice Curriculum schools, the hope will be that students ultimately oversee their own program based on their own interests. When students like Anthony find it difficult to join or remain in the program, possibilities still exist. Teachers, parents, and students within the program can encourage and support those students as deemed fit.

Certainly it is not to be believed that once enrolled in Student Choice Curriculum, a student becomes stable and focused. It is quite possible that by the end of year two, Anthony's interest will shift to Harry Potter, with his studies focused on the history of witchcraft, both the kind where people accused of witchery were burned to death and the fast-growing Wiccan religion. His teachers, having had a set of previous experiences with Anthony, can shape that into something that weaves the Potter series with gaming, playing on the mythical nature J. K. Rowling has woven into her novels.

It may be that by Anthony's third year this may lead him toward some creative ideas about how to design multiple games based on the Potter tales, thereby changing, once again, his focus in math, science, and English. Such a decision may require him to stay for a fourth and maybe even a fifth year, but what's wrong with that? He will graduate as a student who found it difficult to make significant decisions about where his academic interests truly lay, but who ultimately, with the help of teachers, parents, and friends, found a path that took him to an agreed-upon success.

Samantha

Occasionally, you find that high school student who can only be described as brilliant. This kid works well in all subject areas, keeps up to date on current events, and has well-formed opinions on multiple topics. If you've taught long enough, you have encountered one or two of these kids, and they offer as many problems as they do pleasures in the classroom. Such outliers make teaching to the middle of abilities nearly impossible; they also play havoc with differentiating instruction so all students get a fair challenge from the lessons at hand.

The idea that such students will serve as models for the others, showing what exemplary work can look like, works only to a point. Usually that point ends whenever another student has to follow the brilliant one for the delivery of an oral presentation that every student in class knows should have been filmed at the last TED Talks. Brilliant high school students often do not belong in high school classrooms. But there are good arguments that they are not quite ready to be moved into college just yet. How should our schools serve these students? How do you teach those who seem to learn so easily?

Student Choice Curriculum may be as good a way to accomplish those tasks as can be imagined. It's important to think about one such student, Samantha, a third-year student.

Samantha scored at the very top of Duke's Talent Search, though unlike most high-scoring seventh graders, Samantha's score came when she was a sixth grader, as one of her teachers knew the ropes and got her in early. Samantha attended the summer program, and she blew the minds of the educators there.

An avid reader and writer, she has won local school-based poetry contests nearly every year. She published a book of poems in the eighth grade, and in the ninth grade she made a CD of her own songs—she's an excellent guitar player. Her teachers know her to love the writing process, and this year she'll finish her third novel in the NaNoWriMo competition.

She was allowed to grade skip in math to the point where her middle school solicited the help of the director of the math department at the local state college. He came to Samantha's school twice a week to provide focused tutoring that no high school in the area could provide. At her Student Choice School, she is allowed to drive herself to the college campus to continue that exploratory enrichment.

She has read extensively in the realm of women's rights, including Wollstonecraft, de Beauvoir, Belenky, Gilligan, Solnit, and Murdoch.

She was the runner-up in the Siemens Competition, having designed a computer simulation that helped create better communication systems regarding the real-time science of global climate change. The findings, she felt, would help the message of global climate change reach more people and have more influence.

She is fluent in three languages, has won awards in photography, and volunteers nearly eight hours every week at the cancer ward at her local hospital.

Well, you get the picture.

Will Student Choice Curriculum work for Samantha?

Considering the talent within this young person, Student Choice Curriculum may be the only way we could keep such a student motivated in a high school program. Knowing that the system allows her to navigate her own path, create her own learning program, and designate how that program will be conducted and evaluated, Samantha will benefit from the self-directed nature of the learning, allowing her to measure her plans and successes (and failures—she's not perfect) against the models she has set for herself in her design of study.

Because of her talent, teachers will take more opportunities to step back and watch, tweaking only when necessary, accepting that this is a learner who already has a package of great skills, but who needs the human sense of how to use it, a sense that often improves with age and proper mentoring. The chief function of the staff for Samantha's program will be to establish connections with authentic practitioners in the community, people who work in the worlds where Samantha one day hopes to thrive.

She'll be linked with local writers who have published and local women's rights advocates who have links to political figures up to the national level. Perhaps Samantha will need an advocate as she probes the possibilities of postsecondary learning. Such a young mind will draw the attention of many great national and international colleges. Certainly she will benefit from conversations with adults from many walks of life as she makes her choices and negotiates that experience.

Any other educational experience—normal high school, dual enrollment, early college admission—will serve her poorly because she will not be the center of that experience. In Student Choice Curriculum, teachers and students can decide how much intervention and guidance will be needed by the student as she matriculates through the years. Samantha may come with skills already in place, but she still deserves to be challenged properly in ways that will grow her skills. And she still deserves a say in that process. In any other program, she will not have that control, and much of her need to develop as an autonomous learner may be lost.

David

David dreams of owning his own restaurant. This comes, in part, from his parents' love of food, but more from his uncle's work as a chef in a highly regarded, eclectic restaurant in a large city. David has worked there some, bussing tables, and he loves the atmosphere, loves the interaction with the other employees. They know him as the nephew from out of town, but they treat him well and encourage him to keep at it. They all know that a person with restaurant skills can work anywhere. It's a perfectly portable job.

As a child of foodies, David is familiar with much about the culinary experience his classmates miss. His bag lunches are veritable feasts compared to what his friends bring to school. Their packaged meals pale in comparison to his cucumber sandwich with chipotle-flavored mayonnaise on artisan rye with two dill pickles on the side, washed down with homemade ginger water. To his friends' delight, David often invites them in small groups so he can cook for them. He has dabbled in myriad national cuisines and is always looking for ways to bring a new food or preparation to his repertoire.

He makes a variety of paella, several styles of curry chicken or beef, and he cooks a seasoned leg of lamb to perfection. He loves to mix his root vegetables so that potatoes get mashed with carrots, beets with rutabaga, and daikon with butternut squash, that last one totally surprising his uncle into serving it one night at the restaurant. But his favorite work is with soups, and David has set a goal of becoming a stellar soup maker.

Last spring David agreed to cook for six on the night of the prom and offered a contest to those who were interested: they suggested a meal for them and their date and David received twelve entries, from whom he selected the three couples he would feed. Their cost was well below what they would have spent at a restaurant, and David got his parents to work as waitstaff and bussers. It was a tremendous success, and this year he'll be doing it again.

While David loves to work with food, he also knows that owning a restaurant will tax his management skills, especially if it is a place, as is his wish, where he is owner-chef. His uncle went that route once before and found it too much for him to handle. He is now a chef-for-hire—a good one. He makes a comfortable living, but he is quick to remind David that a time did exist when he was close to bankruptcy and wondered how he would pay his staff at the end of the week.

Consequently, part of David's study is focused hard on the mathematics of budgets and financial investment. He wants to know how to work with a particular business plan within a particular geographic region and make ends meet. His sensibilities are that employees should be well-treated, with benefits that make working there worth their while, but that will mean knowing very clearly how the money works, something his uncle tells him is difficult due to restaurants being dependent on the whims of the public.

This has caused David to work with the psychology teachers as well as creating for himself a consistent appointment with his guidance counselor. He knows he must understand people better than he does, both those he hires and those he serves. As a final element of his "dream job" of owning a restaurant, David believes that businesses should serve their community in ways that go beyond being a business. For a restaurant, David takes that to mean he will offer classes and opportunities for locals—sometimes even the very needy locals—to learn how to make soups, salads, casseroles, and other simple fare.

His parents love this about their son, and they love what the experience with Student Choice Curriculum has done for him. David is often in the cafeteria, helping any way he can, and when other kids have a plan for an event, you can be sure that it's David they contact about the food.

The teachers in David's Student Choice program have grown David's dream by pointing him toward some other parts of the culinary arts world. Food is a commodity, so people must sell it, represent it, and market it. David has been involved in several projects that have a significant business angle to them. Restaurants in all markets get reviewed by knowledgeable reporters whose job it is to eat well and find the strengths and weaknesses across the spectrum of eateries: the white tablecloth, five-star Americana bistro with a wine cellar, as well as the greasy-spoon diner that serves up fried chicken and iced tea.

Thus David is learning to write about food in myriad contexts. And, of course, cookbooks are always popular, with the right ones at the right time becoming more than just eye candy on the dining room server. David knows that Julia Child's *Mastering the Art of French Cooking* took the world by storm. He's cooked many of the recipes and seen the Amy Adams and Meryl Streep movie *Julie & Julia* twice.

Finally, the science department has taken on the task of indoctrinating David into the whims and wonders of nutrition science by focusing his attention this year (his third) on Michael Pollan's work. David has been keeping a food diary, and he has become a constant pain in his friends' necks, reminding them that what they are eating is often not even food, and that they are doing their health a disservice by making those choices.

THE TEACHERS

Describing Student Choice Curriculum teachers beyond writing of their need for creativity and out-of-the-box methodologies seems unnecessary. Good teachers understand the dynamic of classroom instruction. By engaging the learning natures of their students, good teachers get most students to do more than the student believes is possible. Student Choice Curriculum will seek good teachers. But so do all schools. Thus it would be wrong to believe that Student Choice Curriculum will need a different kind of teacher or that very specialized training will be needed to create teachers who can work in these learning environments.

As with any educational environment, teachers need to be committed to helping kids explore their own interests within the context of an academic setting. They must like the learning process and believe education to be a fountain of youth. It will be important that teachers have a philosophical underpinning, but it need not be Dewey's or Rousseau's or Piaget's or Vygotsky's. Maria Montessori was most right in suggesting that a better sense of what the classroom experience can become often begins in the frameworks of learning and instruction possessed by the teachers in those learning spaces.

If five or six educational philosophies are represented at a Student Choice Curriculum school, all the better, as this will open up some significant conversations between the teachers regarding the progress of the students there, the same kind of conversations needed to explore the potentials of Student Choice Curriculum. But as you got a sense of four students, it is fair to take a minute and meet two of the teachers.

Mr. Cavendish

One of the English teachers who will be involved with improving Lindsey's writing and her skills of personal interaction, especially interviewing, has been teaching for seven years. Mr. Cavendish is presently working on a master's degree in comparative literature through an online program at a university in the Midwest. He is not a basketball player, though he likes the game, especially the college game when it gets to the final sixty-four. In that light, you might say he's a media junkie.

His greatest asset is flexibility, which makes him perfect for Student Choice Curriculum. Over his short years in the classroom, Mr. C has learned to teach the novel not by having classes read one text together at the same time but rather by letting students select titles from five similar works, and then taking them through the generalities of that particular literary moment or genre. Students conference with him and their peers about the ways their particular books exemplify the literary conventions the class is exploring. He does the same with his studies of poetry and short stories, opting to explore single works only when the class studies drama.

He enjoys the writing process and has attempted to get his work published, finding small success online, something that makes him feel less of a published writer and more of an opportunist. Still, he writes often, keeping himself on a one-thousand-words-per-day regimen. Thus he knows how writing serves the thinking mind, and he encourages his students to create writing habits so they too will understand that writing is a learning tool.

He will finish his master's degree work, and it will inform his teaching in multiple ways, but mostly as a resource for added titles to the choice work he gives his students in literature. He foresees a day when he'll be teaching narrative voice, character development, and the role subcharacter conflicts play in plot development to twenty-three kids who are reading twenty-three different books. His students will learn the material by sharing elements of their novels with other students, using cooperative strategies that capitalize on the social network that is the learning environment.

Collegially, Mr. Cavendish encourages Student Choice Curriculum as he finds the creative energy enjoyable. He likes how it can turn the process and diligence back to the students, who, after all, made their choice to be there on their own.

As other teachers wonder about the times when students were taught the "classics," he reminds them that literary thought is about exploring and knowing the self, and so long as a reader can find personal insights within a text, the goals of literature can be met. Thus, reading Brontë's *Jane Eyre* is no more compelling than reading Bonnie Jo Campbell's *Once Upon a River*: both provide the reader with a strong, independent-minded female protagonist who undergoes significant life lessons and comes out in the end a better human being.

Mrs. Butters

One of the history teachers is a basketball fanatic who played in high school and then went to the University of Kentucky, not to play but to be connected with a college that plays world-class college basketball. Even before working in Student Choice Curriculum, Mrs. Butters encouraged and challenged many of her students to create fantasy basketball teams and to compete as a league for a season. She's been in the classroom for thirteen years and is the history department chair. Her interest in the game has kept her close to the coaching staff and she has occasionally done some scouting for them.

Mrs. Butters's history focus is contemporary European, though she has a personal interest in the expansion of the Roman Empire and the building of Hadrian's Wall, which she has visited twice, one time camping illegally at Harlow Hill. She hasn't written much since college, but she does keep up with her subject area by attending local, state, and (sometimes) National Council for History Education conferences. She has chaired her state's History Council.

Socratic circles and seminars are where Butters's teaching gets its main methodology. She uses these at least three times each grading period, demanding that students come prepared to "do battle" with the ideas of the session. Much work is done to habituate students to the process, showing them how to challenge each other, how to frame good questions, and how to build upon earlier ideas so that a developmental intention can be seen in their overall performance in the circle. She also makes it very clear how their grades will be greatly influenced by those learned skills.

Recently Mrs. Butters started developing authentic Socratic circles where people from the community prepare for and attend an evening circle that students can watch—and the bolder ones can join. Often these are academic sessions, focused on areas in which people maintain interest even if they no longer study the subject: the Civil War, both world wars, natural science, specific art, or voyages of exploration are subjects she has used. But she has also created them as civic expressions and so the issue of a small town's move to adopt an elected mayor instead of, say, an appointed city manager has been something brought before her students.

A ready mind is a better mind, she believes, with ready meaning both preparation for the next level of study and the participatory skills needed in contemporary society. She runs her classes so students learn to behave in that light.

GENERAL THOUGHTS ON TEACHERS

The successful teacher in Student Choice Curriculum will be one who not only has a broad understanding of pedagogical methods, but who also has a keen interest in her subject area. This is, of course, no different from how we would like to describe working teachers in all schools. High school principals from vastly different geographic regions and school types will talk as one when they discuss the skills they seek in new hires: subject knowledge, creativity energy, willingness to differentiate, and a contagious excitability.

That list cannot be improved upon. Good teachers motivate intellectual interaction. Good teaching engenders impromptu visits from a student when classes are not in session. This shows the student's interest in the learning process, and it allows a teacher to prime that interest and suggest a book or an experiment or some other learning opportunity. In Student Choice Curriculum, the teacher always looks for ways to get the student to step into the learning just a bit further, to explore a bit deeper, and to reflect upon the process more critically. In that light, the teacher will have to be a pretty good judge of character.

In other words, Student Choice Curriculum is looking for the same kind of good teachers as every school in our nation, believing that the difference won't be in the skills brought to the classroom but rather how those skills assimilate the learning needs of the students.

In subjects where many educators believe facts and formulae predominate—math and science—teachers will need multiple methodologies to bring those facts and figures to students of a wide range of interests. Statistics won't be taught, nor the natural sciences, as subject areas per se, but rather as methods of thought and application within topics like basketball, video game design, restaurant ownership, and music theory. Teachers will always need to be on the lookout for how their subject is used within those areas of interest students are exploring.

Student Choice Curriculum will focus on dedicated applications within structured human practices. In other words, teachers will need to know how their subject opens up avenues of understanding for real people in the real world. This is not a simple task. Much goes on in the minds of many when they read how CO_2 parts per million inched over 300 in 1950 and have been on a steady rise since, now at just over 400. Understanding the magnitude of these numbers is important, and this hints at the kinds of teachers Student Choice Curriculum schools will need.

As a student, Lindsey will need to develop a wide array of mathematical skills to grow her understanding of particulars and generalities within basketball teams, games, and leagues. Her teachers will need to deal with those data as well, even if their preference is not for the sport. David, Anthony, and Samantha will explore similar mathematical skills, though those skills will be applied to different interest areas, creating different needs for thinking about them. Consequently, those same math teachers will need an ability to dabble in math of every shade and color.

Student Choice Curriculum will not be structured around algebra, geometry, trigonometry, and calculus, even as methods and practices within those subjects will be taught regularly; rather math will be taught from a broader-based perspective. While it is possible a student may choose calculus as her topic area and thus be focused on that particular field, the general presentation of math will be through applications the student can expect in their chosen topic area. In short, math teachers will need to be highly skilled and very interested in the nuances of their field.

The same must be said for science, which will not be structured in the "normal" biology, chemistry, physics, or earth science framework, unless, of course, the student chooses one of those fields. She might choose astronomy or marine biology or plant pathology, thereby forcing a need for flexibility in the science department. Consequently, teachers in Student Choice Curriculum will need to understand the nature of the bottom-up learning paradigm they are creating. This can be a difficult task for some.

The ever-present stereotype of the classroom teacher who has used the same lesson plans for the past twenty years is true only to a small degree. Most high school teachers of math and science—of every subject—love their work so much, field-based curiosities ooze out of them. They take notice when a curious mind begins to emerge in their classroom and they can match that curiosity with an engaging energy in their lessons. Students love the classes those teachers lead, and those teachers love to push their students. It will not be hard to encourage those teachers to take on Student Choice Curriculum classrooms.

Student Choice Curriculum teachers will need to be generalists more than specialists. That doesn't mean a school should not hire a biology major, but rather that the teacher who has made biology her specialty should be aware she'll be teaching science with a capital "S," though she can still emphasize biological processes when they fit within the students' chosen subjects. The same must be true with all Student Choice teachers. (It should be true of all working high school teachers.)

Don't miss this point. Far too often, when pen hits paper to describe preferable teaching practice, ideologues point to teachers who preside in a Socratic stance or who motivate students to go far beyond their skill level and accomplish great things. Such stereotypes are hard to break as well as hard to follow. In truth, high school teaching has little to do with Socratic seminars or Mr. Keating–like activities where students rip introductions from textbooks to understand the importance of thinking for themselves.

Robin Williams's portrayal of a motivating teacher may be universally admired (though Kevin Kline's Mr. Hundert from *The Emperor's Club* is a better model), but so long as the teacher understands that lecturing cannot accomplish as much for the student as active learning, and that over time efforts must be made to know how each student connects to the processes of learning they are exploring, much good will come of those learning interactions.

Student Choice Curriculum recognizes that all learners have interests that will facilitate the intellectual work they need to explore to be good learners. Thus a clever and creative teacher need only begin the process of introducing skill sets and practice activities to get the ball rolling. This does not mean the student does the rest, but that together teacher and student then find ways to explore and uncover new elements of the process that lead toward deeper understanding.

Student Choice Curriculum can succeed with nearly all teachers presently working in classrooms, provided they are nurtured and encouraged toward the different kind of paradigms of learning described in this book. Most teachers want their students to be successful; most love the classroom experience. Give them the chance to combine that experience with the qualities suggested within Student Choice Curriculum, and most teachers will navigate a path toward the necessary skill set.

The conversations these teachers have about a student teetering on the edge of success, the edge that might allow the student to stay in Student Choice Curriculum, but may also mean a reassignment back to the traditional high school curriculum, should be informative as to how this program could work. As described earlier, Michelle Butters teaches history; Marcus Cavendish teaches English. The following conversation concerns Anthony, the first-year student described earlier who was allowed into Student Choice Curriculum in the second grading period.

You'll recall that he hadn't been prepared enough at the end of the third week of school to be enrolled in the first grading period, but through encouragement of friends and acknowledgment of teachers he moved into the program in the second week of the second trimester. It is roughly week nine of the second trimester.

Marcus: Hey Chelle, do you have a few minutes to talk about Anthony?

Michelle: Yeah, absolutely. I saw your email and wanted to get back to you today or tomorrow. Are you ready now?

Marcus: Yeah, I've got some time before I have to monitor the Quiet Chambers in the English hall.

Michelle: Me too. What are you thinking?

Marcus: I'm beginning to see a waning in Anthony's motivation; he's just not making the same kind of effort he did when we moved him over from traditional. He seemed pretty lit up about it then, especially in his exploration of how stories might be used to feed the fictional world of a video game. His reworking of some of Poe's tales went really well. His idea with "The Cask of Amontillado" was excellent, and he was going pretty well with "The Pit and the Pendulum." But now, a lot of that seems to be stopping.

Michelle: He's just fourteen, M. It's hard for first-year kids to keep up a level of energy. You know that.

Marcus: Yeah, that's true. But can you tell me he's still plugging away with your history work? It almost seems like he doesn't even care about the topic anymore.

Michelle: Wow. No. I'm not seeing that, at least not what I'd call losing interest in the topic. But you may be right about him losing energy. I had Anthony in his traditional class in the first grading period. He didn't set the world on fire, but he did his work. Of course, we were looking at colonization and it doesn't generally hold up as the most exciting time of the year for the kids. But, tell me, what are you thinking? Are we wondering if he should stay in Choice?

Marcus: I don't know, and that's why I'm trying to get with all his teachers. I know his parents a little bit. We all work out at the same gym, and they were pretty pleased when Anthony moved into the program. The other night they asked me what I was seeing, because lately, they said, he wasn't doing as much schoolwork at home, but he wasn't playing his games as much either. I told them what I thought, that he'd dropped off some, but I added that as a newbie in the program, especially one who entered midyear, there were different pressures he was facing. I kind of encouraged them that he'd be okay, but I'm not so sure.

Here's the thing, I was supposed to get a paper from him, a kind of storyboard for another Poe story, and we were going to find a way to link him with the computer programmers for this one, so I figured he'd be all for it. But I haven't seen the story.

Michelle: *You think he's blowing it off? Or is it that this is just a bit harder and he's struggling with the challenge?*

Marcus: *I do. He was also supposed to have a major presentation ready by Monday on how stories feed the gaming world. I have arranged for Bruce McDonald to be here.*

Michelle: *Who's that?*

Marcus: *He runs the Escape Room downtown, and he's done some pretty reasonable game design of his own. I'm probably going to have to cancel that, and I hate doing that with our authentic audiences. It's hard enough sometimes just getting them interested, so when a kid doesn't come through, it makes the next time more difficult.*

Michelle: *Can you put Anthony in front of him anyway?*

Marcus: *I don't know. Like I said, he was pretty good with the earlier Poe, so I just figured this would be a good one. But when we talked yesterday, he had nothing ready.*

Michelle: *What story is he working on?*

Marcus: *"Berenice."*

Michelle: *Cool. I love that story. Kind of "Tell-Tale Heart" with a twist.*

Marcus: *Yeah. Me too. But if he's got nothing to show, then I've wasted Bruce's time. I'm just not willing to do that. So what's he doing with your work? You said you had him in Tri One; has he been different? Is he developing the independence we need?*

Michelle: *You know, that's a good question. I guess I don't know, M. I've got him involved in some of the early gaming history, trying to establish a kind of time line of the technology and how it developed an audience. A kind of how-this-happened-when-it-did exploration. He's reading, or at least looking at,* Donovan's Replay, *but it's a tome, almost five hundred pages, and no first-year kid wants to read something like that. He is reading, I mean I think he is really reading,* Masters of Doom, *and that's a good text for his investigation.*

In fact, they're both good histories, and he's talked to me about them and their context, and I've put him in touch with a friend of mine at the Arcade Museum to get a better sense of the context of games over time. I even think, if he wanted, he could get a job there, but I don't know about that. Still, I guess, now that I'm thinking about it, I don't really hear him internalizing any of this right now. And

I was supposed to see that timeline early this week and it hasn't materialized. I guess I'm not seeing the interest either.

Marcus: *That's what I'm thinking, too. He's bright enough, and he's a great gamer by all the reports of his friends. And I think he writes well enough and has a good sense of how this could work to warrant our placement in the program, but he's just not pushing himself, not self-motivating toward the goals he set. He's one short on the Poe stories, and he was also supposed to read Cline's* Ready Player One, *but I don't think he has.*

I think he's found a set of reader's notes and skipped the text. I mean the other day in the Social Hall I was monitor and I put him with David and Lindsey, two pretty good kids, trying to get them to explore how interest opens up investigation. Those two could talk and talk about their love of food and basketball, and especially about the books they were reading—and not just topical reads. But Anthony just listened, barely getting involved, almost nothing to say. Then when David found out Anthony had been reading Ready Player One, *he lit up because he had read the book and loved it.*

He started talking about how some restaurants perform dinner theater, and that there would be no reason why a restaurant couldn't create things like game night with a sort of scavenger hunt theme like with the Easter egg in the novel. I'm telling you, Chelle, it was just like what we hope those Social Halls work up in kids. It was way cool because those other two got some insights about their own abilities to dig into their interest, even how to expand it, and it left me thinking that Anthony is falling victim to the first-year doldrums. He just couldn't keep up.

This week I'm asking him to read another book that I don't think he'll be able to find the notes as easily, just to see how he handles the reading. I've got to get a sense of where he is here. I mean it might be that he's just bored with what I'm assigning him and that we have to ramp things up a bit.

Michelle: *What book? Do I know it?*

Marcus: Erebos? *I'm just reading it now, so I can't tell you much about it. It's a translation from the German, so it can work in some multiple ways, including some cultural aspects of the program. Anthony is taking German, so there's a fit there, and his German teacher told me that Anthony is fine in his language and culture class. The book won some awards when it was first published. I'm literally only eighteen or twenty pages in.*

Michelle: *How'd you find it?*

Marcus: *I asked Bruce McDonald about a good read for a bright kid, and he didn't hesitate. I'm not even sure if I'm going to like it; it's hard sometimes for me to read an adolescent text, but I want to see what Anthony can do. When I'm almost done reading, I'm going to give it to him.*

Michelle: *That's a good idea. What are you hearing from the other teachers?*

Marcus: *Similar things. His German teacher says he's fine; Indira thinks his math skills are on target. Anthony is bright enough, but he's not growing a work ethic, not producing the kind of thoughtfulness and curiosity we hoped for when we let him switch from Traditional.*

If I had to decide right now, I'd keep him, but if this trend doesn't change soon, I might change my attitude. At this point, it doesn't do us much good to have students who choose not to meet the goals, and that's what I'm thinking Anthony is doing just now. There's that potential for kids like David and Lindsey to be drawn down toward the mean when kids like Anthony are allowed to stay.

Michelle: *Well, it's hard for some kids. They just don't have the background for personal intellectual investment. And there's just too much white noise surrounding them to allow a clear focus. Keep me posted, M. I'm on board with what you're saying. Almost in the exact same place. I like Anthony, but I'm watching him.*

SCHOOL TO COMMUNITY TO SCHOOL

The teacher who finds the right fit within Student Choice Curriculum can convince people in the community to take an interest in the school's practices. Math and science teachers will need to communicate with professors at the local colleges and universities, as well as with people of the community for whom math is central to their lives. This is less difficult than initially perceived. A simple invitation to an open house for math or science-minded people would gather, at worst, a small crowd from the community.

Energetic faculties of both departments could uncover several new faces ready to help those struggling math and science students at the school. Such people live in our communities; parent-teacher associations and booster clubs demonstrate that communities want education to be effective. With Student Choice Curriculum, the kind of investment may be a bit different, in that the result will be a merging of teacher and community members *in* the classroom.

Thus successful teachers, administrators, and counselors will have to feel comfortable in the community setting, talking with people about how their help can make students' learning experiences more effective. They will have to find and convince people to give time:

- As a member of an authentic audience
- For interactive dialogues with students
- As a guest lecturer or workshop leader

It would be extremely valuable for Lindsey to sit in on an interview workshop conducted by the editor of the sports department of the local newspaper during the school day. If that workshop included the editor actually interviewing a significant personality, all the better.

In Student Choice Curriculum, the teacher must become a more vibrant, interactive member of the local community than is normally understood about our teachers. They must sell the program to the community. Student Choice Curriculum will have to demonstrate to their communities why education matters. It is a system that endeavors to include the community in all that it does.

Moreover, the school must be a place where significant events of the community's decision-making processes occur. Teachers occasionally serve in their town, city, county, or even state political systems. It is rare to find a school that does not have at least one teacher who has been or is serving in an elected position. But even if there are no teachers serving in that capacity, the school should be the site of public meetings from time to time. Student Choice Curriculum schools will always provide opportunities for students to see how community life reinvents itself and to think critically about any community they call home.

Student Choice Curriculum schools will need a community liaison, much like a sales manager, who promotes the school's needs and functions. There are many ways to consider this position, and different communities will define the position differently, but the central task will be for the representative to make herself known in all of the retail stores, restaurants, newspapers, law offices, coffee shops, and other businesses in town. Her face should be immediately known at the hospital, the fire department, the emergency medical responder station, and the police department. If there's a local theater or professional sports team, she should be known there, too.

Many students will seek internships in particular and general circumstances; many will need the benefit of authentic audiences. Someone who knows what the school is doing; someone who knows the workings of the community; some person of viable social and instructional skills will be essential in creating the bridge between school and community.

There is at least one more duty for teachers working at Student Choice Curriculum schools: all will be expected to participate in regular debates with colleagues in scheduled, open-forum real-time demonstrations. This should be a staple of schools already. Teachers are well-educated individuals; many have earned graduate degrees. They can pursue knowledge, they can make and defend arguments within multiple contexts, and they have an experienced perspective upon the communities where they live. Teachers have insights into their communities, and those insights can be put to the test of open debate.

This will clearly be a benefit for students who will watch mental investment in an authentic debate. Within the context of Student Choice Curriculum there should be three debates a year, one in each grading period. Topics will be selected by popular interest, though every effort should be made to include significant local issues along with well-known national or global ones. When the issues have been established, teachers will sign up for topics that interest them, topics they know to be central to their own sense of community importance.

The requirement of participation will depend greatly on the nature of the staff and the size of the school, but it makes sense that each teacher will have to take part in two debates annually—once actively, one as a judge. Each debate will be held in front of a live student and community audience.

Different schools will conduct these debates differently, but they should be fully organized, rule-based debates, with opening statements, challenging questions, and a winner selected by a team of student and teacher judges. This should be a social event, where participants and audience mingle after—in one of the large meeting areas of the school.

Students would be delighted to see their teachers open up on presidential candidates, capital punishment, legalization of marijuana, immigration, health care, abortion, and sundry other topics. Those students who have come to identify with one or two of their teachers will find it fascinating to watch them use their minds to navigate the difficult terrain of a controversial topic. Modeling is one of the central modalities of active instruction, so using teachers to debate particulars in front of a student audience will be a great way to model intellectual mindfulness.

Such an activity would go a long way in transforming a school into a community, a place where all learners, teachers and students alike, have a chance to know each other as learners, as people who deal with the experiences life throws at them. Students don't always know what is in the heads of their teachers, and teachers often share the same lack of their students *and* of other teachers. But each needs some sense of this if learning is to expand and to matter.

Community-building experiences within the context of Student Choice Curriculum will engender learning relationships, opportunities to share life lessons and opinions in both directions, concepts that generally only travel one way in our schools. As students see their teachers support opinions with lived experiences, students will come to understand the differences between opinions and experiences, opening up great learning possibilities for those students.

It should be clear that any school can begin the process of using Student Choice Curriculum with the staff and administration on board right now. Incorporating strategies of working directly with students' interests will demonstrate pretty quickly those teachers who find it invigorating and those who don't. After an introductory period, a core of teachers will be firmly rooted in the Student Choice Curriculum paradigm, and they will shape the program to fit their school and student preferences.

This group will encourage many who are on the fringe but just need a little more experience or opportunity to make it work.

CURRICULAR POTENTIALS

As this chapter has provided a glimpse of the students and teachers who populate a Student Choice Curriculum school, it is also fitting that some overview of potential yearly curricula be offered. Using the students described earlier, what follows is an overview of three years in the program. Keep in mind that all of this is suggestive, not prescriptive. The nature of Student Choice Curriculum makes everything negotiable.

Basketball, the First Year

First-year students will receive a very basic introduction to Student Choice Curriculum, spreading their interest across the traditional academic areas most high schools address. The difference, as has been mentioned in this book, is that significant negotiation between the students and their teachers will shape and reshape the day-to-day delivery of that curriculum.

Lindsey should expect that not many weeks will go by when she is not asked to sit with at least one, and generally several, of her teachers in order to share personal reflections on her progress. Student Choice Curriculum is self-designed, but for the first-year students, much practice in the way of self-evaluation needs to occur. A basic set of resources and activities with the several academic areas for the first-year student studying basketball follows.

Mathematics

For her first year, Lindsey will be focused on the geometry of basketball, including an understanding of the geometric principles of the shapes that appear on the court and how those shapes can be used to prove particular theorems, like corresponding angles postulates or symmetric or transitive properties, or the definition of supplementary and complementary angles.

Projects may include:

- Direct comparisons of floor space for different levels of play—high school, college, and professional courts—and how that changed nature of space changes both the nature of the game and the expected abilities of the players therein. Bigger courts will not only imply greater skills, but quicker, stronger players. A central question might be "how does the nature of the physical court make demands on the players of the game at

that level?" Students will learn a full complement of geometric vocabulary through the study of the court and its changes over the years and across levels of play.
- Design of several courts that demonstrate how the rules of the court matter. To make these designs will require a keen sense of the rules of the game, and this adds to the freshman year, a dedicated focus on the rules of basketball—high school, college, and professional. Within these designs will be considerations of board feet and coating. This project also includes a necessary connection with the visual arts, as issues of team mascots, color blending, and the like will come into play.

Literature/English

For the reading component of Lindsey's first year, she will focus mostly on narratives of basketball's connection with human life. The focus will be on players, and both on- and off-the-court experiences, and how a paradigm of playing basketball seriously helps (or hinders) a person's perspective on life.

Texts might include:

- *The Chance* by Karen Kingsbury
- *True Legend* by Mike Lupica
- *Boy 21* by Matthew Quick
- *That Championship Season* by Jason Miller. It was the recipient of the 1973 Pulitzer Prize for Drama.
- *Jump Ball* by Mel Glenn

Films:

- *Finding Forrester* directed by Gus Van Sant
- *Hoop Dreams* directed by Steve James
- *Love and Basketball* directed by Gina Prince-Bythewood

Projects may include:

- An in-depth exploration of how authors blend the relationship with the game in symbolic representation. The relationships within these novels will be juxtaposed with the relationships of the films.
- Lindsey should expect to write often, including four major papers, each approaching 1,500 words.
- She should also expect to deliver her oral presentations, with at least one of those in front of an authentic audience.

History

Lindsey will look back on basketball as a social phenomenon, focusing on the growth of the game and the changed nature of the players and their needs.
  Texts may include:

- *The Biographical History of Basketball* by Peter Bjarkman
- *Cages to Jump Shots* by Robert Peterson
- *A Season on the Brink* by John Feinstein
- *The City Game* by Pete Axthelm
- *Where the Game Matters Most* by William Gildea

Projects may include:

- A timeline of significant events from basketball's beginning, including some statements that frame causality on changes in the game.
- A major PowerPoint production of "the history of basketball" to be delivered to an authentic audience of players, fans, coaches, and officials (not to be combined with the three presentations in English).
- A major paper that reports on interviews conducted by the student of former players from the high school, modeled on the books read for the class.

Science and Physical Education

Lindsey's approach to science will be an exploration of human physical endurance science coupled with a specific and hands-on physical education study of training procedures. This will be centered on a set of basic questions, from which Lindsey will develop particular and general hypotheses:

- What can the body do as far as physical output is concerned?
- How does particular and general training improve the fitness of a human body?
- When is the body, within the realm of the human life span, at its peak physically?
- Why are these questions important for a beginning understanding of the relationship of science to basketball?

Projects may include:

- A video montage representing basketball players through the ages, depicting the way physicality and athletic training have changed.

Foreign Language, Cultural Studies

As with all the classes mentioned, much of each class will depend on entry-level skills. Far too often students arrive in high school having never taken a foreign language class. Thus, a very basic beginning should be expected in this area. Nevertheless, contemporary technology provides Lindsey opportunities to listen to major basketball broadcasts in the language she is studying. There will be ample opportunities to practice the language in a context she'll find interesting.

Also, as basketball offers its own set of skills, some of them unique to the game, a unique vocabulary is also to be learned in order to understand the game's dimensions. Thus Lindsey will have a reason for growing her foreign language vocabulary in ways that other high school students might not.

Projects may include:

- A creation of a basketball glossary in the language of study
- A comparison of descriptions of similar (or perhaps the exact same) basketball plays in different languages, allowing Lindsey to see how different cultures describe and value different aspects of the game

Music through Guitar, the Second Year

Anthony, you'll remember, became involved in Student Choice Curriculum in the second grading period in his first year of high school, but by year's end he had transitioned back to the traditional program. That summer he began playing guitar and, to his parents' surprise, developed a serious practice habit. All three go to the school a week before the fall session and a plan is created for Anthony to begin his second year studying guitar as a performance instrument.

This works well for the first two grading periods, but during the third grading period, his interest in guitar wanes, and his teachers see it. They work with him to regain his focus, but it is hard. A major parent-teacher-student conference is held where this team of stakeholders explores Anthony's work and interest in order to keep him in Student Choice Curriculum. If they cannot, there is little to expect other than two more years of high school in traditional classes. If they can, Anthony may find himself immersed in another personal interest when the third year begins. Here's what Anthony's musical plan for the second year may look like:

Mathematics and the Arts

Since Pythagoras there has been a demonstrable link between music and math. Moreover, students who are actively pursuing musical expression generally score better in math assessments. Thus, a significant part of Anthony's artistic exploration in this year will be an intensive pursuit of guitar skills. On a daily basis, a qualified music instructor will lead him through many steps of performance skills.

Mathematically, fractions and ratios are obviously important to music, as they frame an understanding of harmony and chord structure. Moreover, pattern recognition is an essential math and music link, so looking into numerical series like Fibonacci numbers should be fruitful. Other links between music and math involve algebra, geometry, rhythm, intervals, time signatures, tone, and pitch, concepts to be built collaboratively by both the music and math instructors.

Anthony will also spend some time with the golden ratio, especially as it helps us to understand humanity's connection with beauty. Music is many things, but for most it is a way to enjoy esthetics in a very personal way. How interesting it will be for Anthony to discover that, in part, such esthetic enjoyment is measurably mathematical.

In Anthony's study of math, it will be important that the music and math teachers work together to frame a cross-curricular approach. Two important, though difficult, texts should inform some of what will occur in Anthony's math:

- *Cool Math for Hot Music* by Guerino Mazzola, Maria Mannone, and Yan Pan Clark
- *Musimathics: The Mathematical Foundations of Music* by Gareth Loy

Projects may include:

- Composing an original piece of music that demonstrates an understanding of the mathematical ideas explored; perform this piece of music in front of students.
- Develop a graphic organizer that presents the musical patterns of different genres of music, with an emphasis on the mathematical aspects of those patterns.
- Linking music and visual beauty through an application of the golden ratio in a stand-alone "station" that will be on display in the Interactive Construction Areas (see chapter 4).

Literature/English

For the reading component of Anthony's second year, he will focus mostly on narratives that weave music into the lives of real characters. The focus will be on how music is a part of life, not necessarily the only part. From these works, Anthony will develop several written works, generally exploring how music is used to intensify the reading experience.

Texts might include:

- *A Visit from the Goon Squad* by Jennifer Egan
- *High Fidelity* by Nick Hornby
- *Bel Canto* by Ann Patchett
- *The Soloist* by Steve Lopez

Films:

- *8 Mile* directed by Curtis Hanson
- *Inside Llewyn Davis* directed by Ethan and Joel Coen
- *Amadeus* directed by Miloš Forman

Projects may include:

- Anthony will be asked to write often in his second year, assuming several different voices in these works. This will include analyses of particular elements of the films and novels, as well as connectives pieces that link styles and themes.
- Create a video montage that demonstrates music's role in many films. This *should not* be a "greatest hits" package but rather a vehicle to show how filmmakers use music to enhance the emotional understanding of the film.
- Anthony should also expect to deliver three oral presentations, with at least one of those in front of an authentic audience of local musicians.

History

It can be expected that Anthony will be enamored of modern music, especially as much of his interest in guitar was fed by YouTube videos in the summer between year one and two. Thus, the history he'll be looking at should be contemporary, though culturally broad.

Anthony's teachers should encourage him to explore outside of his musical interests in ways that offer him an understanding of the rich historical legacy music offers, even if only in a fairly contemporary (twentieth-century) approach.

Texts may include:

- *Freedom of Expression: Interviews with Women in Jazz* by Chris Becker
- *The Rough Guide to World Music: Africa and Middle East* by multiple writers
- *The Rest Is Noise* by Alex Ross

Projects may include:

- A timeline of significant musical events demonstrating how different musical genres evolved and developed in the twentieth century.
- A major paper that reports on interviews conducted by the student of significant local musicians of various instrumentation and musical genres.
- A personal performance, with live annotations, about different playing styles from the beginning of the twentieth century to now.

Science and Physical Education

It seems that very little will occur in physical education applications for music, though Anthony could conduct an exploration on the different ways guitarists play for performance. For example, blues guitarists often sit to play while folk guitarists generally stand. Anthony could approach this physicality in connection to the style of the music.

Scientifically, a significant study on sound, sound waves, and hearing across multiple species would be applicable. Within the context of this exploration, ideas of technology could be investigated especially as they apply to hearing enhancement. Links to other technical prosthetics would be fitting. This will be centered on a set of basic questions, from which Anthony will develop particular and general hypotheses:

- How do the various types of musical instruments create different tonality?
- How are the conditions for optimum sound in, say, a concert auditorium improved?
- How should we understand the hearing proficiency of different species?

Projects may include:

- An audio montage representing myriad sounds from a wide array of animal experience. Part of this project will be to demonstrate the different nature of hearing across species.

Foreign Language, Cultural Studies

As has been mentioned, much of these classes will depend upon entry-level skills. Far too often students arrive in high school having never taken a foreign language class. Thus, a very basic beginning should be expected in this area. Nevertheless, contemporary technology gives Anthony opportunities to listen to a wide array of musical styles and genres; every human culture (though perhaps not subculture) enjoys a variety of music.

As music offers its own set of skills and instrumentation, a unique vocabulary is also to be learned in order to understand this breadth. Consequently, Anthony will have a reason for growing his foreign language vocabulary in ways that other high school students might not.

Projects may include:

- The creation of a musical glossary in the language of study.
- A comparison of similar and different musical preferences by culture. For example, the nature of blues as performed in the Mississippi Delta, Chicago's South Side, and London, England.

Culinary Arts, Third Year

The third year is extremely important for the student involved in Student Choice Curriculum, as it will push the work toward a very independent level of performance. The first two years have been student-centered, and negotiations with teachers have been mandatory at many junctures, as has attendance at all the learning spaces on campus. Students should leave year two with a core package of academic skills in place—the science, the math, the reading/writing, the history, and so on—so the third year becomes the time for the student to show what he can do with those resources.

Within Student Choice Curriculum, the third year has the potential to be the culminating year for many students. Teachers will observe students to spot their independent drive and curiosity, their creation of personal challenges within skill sets, and their ability and willingness to seek assistance when needed. Meetings may be less structured and occur less often, but they will hold more weight.

Students will need to convince many teachers that they are ready to go to work, or onto the next level of significant study, else they will need to have at least one more year at the school. Designing the third year, like all years, will be a shared task between students and teachers, taking place in those first three weeks of school. This overview will focus on David, our culinary arts specialist.

Mathematics

By the third year of the program, the basic elements of the mathematical skills needed within the study should be demonstrable through many student behaviors. We should expect David to be proficient on the kind of math a restaurant owner/chef would need: budget planning, payrolls, food ordering, and projection figures based on current analysis of business. This math would include statistics and algebra as well as some of the math done by economists or accountants that focus on the nature of individual businesses, both over a long period of time and at start-up moments.

Thus, in this year, the math department will almost surely push David to become very "number sound," and to work the functionality of particular math applications in his head, or at least in a kind of real-world approximation that makes sense. This could be done in a number of ways, but one would be to have David create a virtual restaurant and situate that business in a real geographic area. He could do the work to discover the:

- Property rental and tax base
- The cost of renovation
- The manner to get that money in loans or investments by friends
- The actual cost of day-to-day functioning—the business hours and employee circumstances

Moreover, this virtual restaurant could be used to explore how actual business finance functions, with David's math teachers challenging him with hypothetical numbers on different aspects of the business on a weekly basis—dinners, food costs, food spoilage, payroll, weather damage to the physical structure, and so on. This would provide David with a significant exploration on the actual math he might use when he opens a place of his own.

Projects may include:

- Weekly and quarterly reports on the success of the restaurant with an authentic audience who represent both his investors and employees.

Literature/English

American education has long required students to complete four years of "English," though the reasons behind that have not been clear. There may be arguments that surveys of different national literatures allow students to expand and become more sensitive or tolerant to other ways of life, but they are not convincing. Every student reads two or three Shakespeare plays and explores a small range of novels and novelists. Good programs consider the ethnic and cultural background of the authors, but even when things go well, it is hard to see how any high school literature program does service to the reading needs of the student.

By the third year of Student Choice Curriculum, the basic elements of restaurant and food writing will have been introduced, practiced, and polished. If he has not achieved success therein, David will continue work in those practices. Moreover, by the third year David should be well versed in the places where reliable print resources can be found on the nature of restaurant ownership and the culinary arts.

Thus his work in this area will be to select particular readings from multiple genres—food magazine articles, full-length books, blogs, and other pertinent and respected sources—and create an authentic readers' group. The nice part of this work is how it will bring a cross section of both the faculty and people of the community. Foodies exist in every walk of life, so this readers' group will include math, science, history, and psychology teachers from the school, as well as chefs, doctors, electricians, and musicians from outside the school.

Projects may include:

- The development of a curriculum that could be used by others investigating the culinary arts and/or restaurant ownership as their topic of interest in Student Choice Curriculum. This would be a reading list that included significant notations on the readings pointing out why each would be essential to such a study. It would also be good if the readings were ordered chronologically so that a newcomer to the field might be brought up to speed in the right acceleration and context.

History and Science

In David's third year, history and science will combine due to a major project he will undertake. In a green space at the school, David will grow various edible crops in ways that farmers have grown those crops over the years. While it won't be possible for him to experiment too broadly, he will be asked to research the nature of farming in several culinary traditions and to blend what those farmers knew with the science of their time.

Much has changed in the world of farming, and some of it seems to be counterproductive for both the quality and quantity of the food. Certain parts of the farming culture will be investigated in this experiment, to be determined by David and the science teachers.

Foreign Language, Cultural Studies

In his third year, David will be asked to do some significant work translating specific cookbooks, food books, and restaurant books in both directions: native language to learned language; learned language to native language. This will obviously be based on sections and recipes and smaller samplings of the food topic, but it will be broad-based in scope. Food writing is a worldwide phenomenon, and there will be many opportunities for David to find restaurant reviews, recipe books, books on food culture, and various other resources focused on the nature and splendor of food.

Projects may include:

- Written translations of the mentioned work
- Oral presentations of the work in the learned language
- Real-time conversations about food and restaurants with native speakers of the learned language

DOUBLING DOWN ON THE MAJOR ISSUES

1. Human intellectual endeavors expand human potential, so educational energy should be invested into the creative capacities of all students.
2. Students will find educational dedication to be more easily mustered in Student Choice Curriculum due to the element of personal choice of the topics being studied.
3. Because good teachers already differentiate instruction and encourage students to go "beyond the lesson," Student Choice Curriculum doesn't require a retooling of the teachers' skill sets.
4. Student Choice Curriculum teachers are flexible, pedagogically rich generalists more than specialists; they possess internalized understanding of how their subject area addresses specific learning needs in the real world.
5. Student Choice Curriculum will help students appreciate the purpose behind educational engagements better than current educational practices do.
6. All Student Choice Curriculum teachers will need to play a role in formal debates, thus serving as models for addressing public and controversial issues in our communities.
7. In the negotiated space Student Choice Curriculum creates, student choice can be "tweaked" by the school, provided the alteration process includes the significant stakeholders in the student's education plan—student, parents, teachers, and counselors.

8. Student Choice Curriculum will make continual educational links with the local community, providing students with learning tasks that reveal how particular and purposeful learning always connects with a community's needs.
9. Student Choice Curriculum will break the traditional four-year matriculation of high schools, sometimes graduating a student early, sometimes requiring the student to stay on for extra time.

Chapter 4

Putting the Program into Practice

One never learns to understand truly anything but what one loves.

—Goethe

FRAMING THOUGHTS

To what degree do you seek to be a part of the processes you engage with, and to what degree do you want someone "above" you to tell you what to do and how to do it? How do these differences manifest in the outcomes you attain? These are the core questions you should be exploring as you engage with this chapter. Teachers have always held stereotypical roles. What would happen if those roles were changed? When you consider your time in high school, perhaps you recall an event or a person who allowed you to experience the kind of empowerment that choice can engender. Let that be a guiding force for the reading here. Moreover, though this book has been about the high school experience, what about it might be spread across all educational paradigms? In other words, how might choice be offered to all students at all grade levels?

The idea of allowing students to organize their entire educational experience around personal interest is counterintuitive to the way most people understand education. For those people, education occurs when someone who knows something shares that knowledge with another person who it is believed needs to know that same thing. These people imagine the need to bisect an angle or conjugate a verb or summarize the content of the Bill of Rights to be self-evident. Moreover, they believe addressing these concepts is the essence of classroom learning, and that such lessons be repeated and drilled yearly until a minimum score is obtained on a test.

In this paradigm education is a top-down process that places the teacher and learner on different planes. Learning experiences are designed by the teacher, then presented to group learners. This process is thought to be efficient in that it defines a needed skill, frames that skill within a particular pedagogic approach, and then engages selected students through the functions of that pedagogy. This image accepts the metaphor that the teacher passes down important information to awaiting minds. Enlightenment, in this metaphor, always comes from above.

Of course, part of this metaphor works well enough. Generally speaking, teachers know their subject area better than the students they teach. Teachers have more flexibility in the conceptual applications of their knowledge, thus when students confront obstacles to learning, teachers ought to be more adept in developing methods of presenting difficult material. The metaphor presents the teacher-as-guru sitting atop the learning pyramid ready to bestow upon the learner powerful and important knowledge. We should look more closely at this metaphor, for it is not the image from which educational success derives.

MOTIVATION AND GURUS

When dealing with gurus or spiritual teachings they deliver, stories relate how a novice goes directly to the guru, often by climbing a mountain or discovering some secret path or overcoming some obstacle, with a particular question to ask of the guru. The process is never that the guru, knowing what we most desperately need, comes down from the mountain to bestow knowledge upon us. Gurus lie in waiting. They may have what is wanted, but people must be savvy and worthy to get them to share it.

To benefit from a guru, you must know how to ask, even if you don't know exactly how it might help you or even what it might be in the first place.

You might not be able to name the quality initially; you might not know the source for its inspiration; but most people recognize the need to know a particular kind of knowledge about a particular kind of topic. When that occurs to us, we seek help or guidance—we find a guru.

The metaphor is good for education, for sometimes an incidental occurrence begets the need of a guru. For example, how many young children dream of becoming a magician after that first experience of a live magic show? These children then seek out a how-to-do-magic book, or these days, search YouTube to learn some sleight-of-hand crafts.

How many youth imagine themselves on the court or field or ice after their first experience at a sporting event? They follow this experience with a request for a ball and that a hoop might be mounted on the garage, hoping Mom or Dad will play with them and teach them the skills of the game.

And how many people woke up Monday morning, February 10, 1964, and combed their hair quite differently after seeing the Beatles on *The Ed Sullivan Show* the night before? With guitars and stardom in their heads, many signed up for music lessons.

People can't always know what their motivations will be, but myriad lives attest to the fact that time and again, personal interests motivate the need to learn something new, something exciting, something that will change the nature of our living conditions. Unquestionably, people like those moments.

Schools, rather than delivering knowledge in their top-down fashion, should capitalize on student curiosity and situate themselves as the guru students seek. Stimuli that promote learning and curiosity create needs in students to the point where they have self-motivated toward digital tutorials of a wide variety. It should be easy for schools to become a place where students explore new avenues and possibilities just as quickly as they materialize in the young learners' minds. Indeed, there should be no better place to do this than at a school, and it is tantamount to malpractice when education does not avail learners of this possibility.

Schools abuse the guru metaphor by believing they not only have what students need, but also that they will make sure students receive it. Thus, they don't dignify the role of student motivation in the process. Everything is done from a top-down paradigm, where the metaphor of the guru must include a climb that goes from the bottom up.

The real problem with top-down learning is that it rarely informs how or why the knowledge is important. Learning that descends from teacher to student without regarding and engaging her interests misses significant opportunities for the student to connect learning and life. Top-down learning assumes a faulty paradigm of learning and thereby begins the process of instruction on the wrong foot. Education is an inductive, bottom-up process that manifests itself regularly in a normal human life.

PARADIGM SHIFT

Believing that students should not be able to choose what and how they study misses the whole point of education. This is the biggest paradigm shift within Student Choice Curriculum. Education must come from the bottom up, in a shared process that explores and reflects upon the interests of both the learner and the teacher. Learners discern what they need to know and teachers help them engage with that process. Lindsey's study of basketball will involve a reinvention of her educational paradigm while she simultaneously designs it in real time.

Student Choice Curriculum will redesign the meeting places in which education occurs. Teachers no longer will design lessons based solely on what they believe students must learn of their topic; rather they will shape each student's learning based on goals and terms negotiated by the student and teacher. Students no longer will receive a syllabus outlining the course of study for the next so many weeks; rather they will explore their chosen interest for ways to match it with the academic subject of study.

Creative individuals talk about such design as akin to building a bicycle while that bicycle is being ridden. It is a highly functional metaphor. As Lindsey moves through her self-created curricula, she will encounter new learning terrain and techniques, which may require new tires or different gear ratios for climbing the hills that she, herself, is discovering. As her ride continues, she might even discover that the old myth of one never forgetting how to ride a bicycle may be a damaging thought. Lindsey may need to reimagine her entire approach to riding a bicycle if she really wants to ride it well.

However, changing the approach to learning is antithetical to what most contemporary schools do. In today's high schools, teachers can fairly assume far ahead of time what a new ninth grader's four years will be like, year to year, class to class. Once the initial elective is selected, the matriculation becomes clearer. This stepwise approach negates a learner's creativity and fails to coordinate intellectual growth with new and specific challenges. It is a bicycle built long ago.

Student Choice Curriculum will change that through the ongoing negotiations that occur between students and teachers, building a system that dignifies the learner and the learning that consistently serve to change educational goals. With the student in charge of what will be studied and how it will be assessed, Student Choice Curriculum changes the basic design and direction of institutional learning.

Such changes, like building a moving bicycle, are not always easy to apprehend or implement. But they are necessary if we want our educational system to develop minds that are more adept in finding and solving important problems. The ride of a quality education frees the mind to think on its own; such a ride must be self-directed in nearly every way, though it is reasonable to include a coordinator who helps in the construction of a good map.

American education has pedaled too long in one big circle, on the wrong bicycle, imagining the journey has been for the good. But it has not. That American education is serving its students or the world well is no longer supportable. The current status of American political behavior says much about our nation's education. Too many politicians do not believe in man-made global climate change or evolutionary biology or the ills created by our enormous wealth gap. The paradigms of American education are not serving the world or its citizens; they do not promote the critical thinking necessary for living in a complex world.

If today's educational policies continue, especially the misguided idea that school choice is an economic and not a learning issue, public education will go the way of landline phones. Practices in our schools must change and students' interests must be respected; to think otherwise is to miss the point of education's tremendous disconnect with reality. Student Choice Curriculum offers some ideas for creating significant changes, one of the first being to change the core nature of the student-teacher relationship.

LEARNING RELATIONSHIPS

It is largely accepted that the teacher-student relationship is central to all things good in the educational process. Good parents want teachers who take time to know their children and who work daily to develop personalized and differentiated instruction. Good teachers want parents who encourage their children to study hard and take educational experiences seriously. Good parents visit schools often, providing and receiving insights on the progress (and lack thereof) of their children. Good students want teachers to be cordial but firm, informative without being too intellectual, and able to understand the nature of student life in the modern world.

Every stakeholder in this blended concoction of interacting minds and motivations knows that relationships—parent/teacher; teacher/student; student/teacher; parent/child—make a difference in educational experiences. None of this is debated in the educational literature, not from the unions or the think tanks or any of the teacher workrooms around the country. Learning relationships matter. Good teachers teach more than their subject; good students learn more than they are taught; good parents foster more than just positive attitudes in their children.

But this thinking errs in assuming a paradigm that too often goes unspoken, and thus unheard. The idea of something being right comes at us through a bygone language that misrepresents the purpose of the task at hand. The error is simple in its stating, a mere change of phrase amends it; but this phrase represents something vastly different from what most understand education to be today.

Student Choice Curriculum will change the basic educational paradigm from a teacher/student relationship to the more powerful learner/learner relationship. In Student Choice Curriculum, both the teacher and the student will need to understand themselves and each other as pivotal partners in what is being learned in both the classroom and the larger, community-based learning environment. Lindsey and her teachers will need to know that during the process that opens up her exploration of basketball, both will discover new truths about their world.

For Lindsey it will be the worlds of basketball and of personal academic commitment; for her teachers it will be the worlds of pedagogy and how personal interest motivates methodologies and outcomes. With both stakeholders functioning as learners, both will actively question the process of exploration. Lindsey may ponder how to write proper questions for different interviews, regarding the various experiences of the interviewee, and how subtle connections can be forged through different questioning content.

Simultaneously, her teacher may reflect on how to ramp up the level of authentic audiences so that Lindsey's interviews will be akin to real-world broadcast or print journalism. Student learners are focused on what they want to learn, while teacher learners are focused on how learning environments must adapt to learners and their personally constructed explorations. If they do their jobs intentionally, striving for excellence, both will be better: the student will be more able to internalize and transfer her learning of the interview process, while the teacher will be able to help other learners gain more from the challenge of authentic audiences.

This kind of procedural growth does not happen in the current paradigm of education, though not for the lack of teacher skill or will. Because of the failure of curricular structure, graduation requirements, and the lack of seeking student interest in the first place, dual learning and responsibility does not occur. Moreover, as current educational practices push students toward the same standardized goals so to pass the same standardized test, there is little incentive for teachers to invest intellectual interest in any one student's educational journey.

Student Choice Curriculum functions through a process most of us have experienced by working in the real world. Colleagues share and construct new ideas within the frameworks of particular and general challenges offered in work environments. Families also recognize this process in the way they address situations that arise at home. Problems are confronted, questions get asked, and ideas are put into the service of discovery.

People involved in life attempt to solve the problems that confront them, especially when those problems arise within parameters that hold their interest. Often this includes new learning, because new learning can provide opportunities for a better life. Human beings are learners all the time. And they like it. Student Choice Curriculum will tap into that nature and bring it to the classroom.

Within a learner-learner paradigm, the classroom will feel different than it does in the teacher-student paradigm. In the former, both stakeholders construct ways to accomplish tasks of interest; both explore the changing nature of those tasks even as they are being accomplished.

Consider Lindsey's exploration of a current controversy of college athletics: the big money received by schools but the zero monetary profit received by players, even though it is their talent and charisma that creates the boon for their athletic departments. In a learner-learner relationship, both Lindsey and her teacher must take part in the negotiations that detail the kind of work Lindsey will complete. As both are stakeholders in this intellectual development, both learn how to navigate the terrain.

Lindsey will be encouraged to investigate, coordinate, evaluate, and present information about the controversy, while her teacher will need to expand and explore the nature of interactive teaching that includes both the student and the community. Lindsey will want to work one way; her teacher may suggest another. There is no right way or set path for this learning to occur, and similar interactions across the student enrollment will all be different.

Each learner will learn from the other. The teacher adjusts the learning environment to enhance Lindsey's motivation, concurrent with discovering what Lindsey's mind can do. This process could change daily in a smooth, evolutionary process, though it is probably better to think of the changes as coming in a more punctuated fashion, with each negotiation session. There will be resources to suggest, methods of critical thinking the teacher can model, and there will be time-management strategies that can help Lindsey through the process of exploring this who-gets-the-money controversy.

Simultaneously, Lindsey will be discovering how her interest in basketball allows her to see into other issues connected to the sport she loves. She can compare her understanding of the game at one level while exploring a controversy at another. This should create some moments of significant insight, and Lindsey will almost surely begin to connect pertinent applications of, say, capitalism, with basketball at all levels. This will lead her to new questions, not only about the game she loves, but also about the social world in which she and that game exist.

Thus, with the modeling and direction her teacher is offering, Lindsey's interest will be reengaged by a set of new challenges on a regular basis. It will be hard work, as her teacher will be moving Lindsey's zone of proximal development higher and higher; but it will also be hard for Lindsey to refuse these pushes, as she loves the game, and so the work remains motivating. Through a continual measuring of the intellectual growth of her student, Lindsey's teacher is becoming better at her craft. As Lindsey is discovering what it means and how it feels to be pushed in the most positive ways, she is becoming a better student.

Regarding the who-gets-the-money controversy, for example, if Lindsey finds this to be a fruitful area of research, her teacher might want her to investigate the notorious Fab Five of Michigan, 1991, 1992, and 1993, and how they changed the way the University of Michigan paid for, and was rewarded for, their basketball program. It is imaginable Lindsey has never heard the names of Rose, Webber, Howard, King, and Jackson, so the teacher's experience becomes a part of the student's exploration.

Note that this can come about in two ways:

- The teacher recalls the situation at Michigan from the early 1990s.
- The teacher does some particular research herself to find new avenues of challenge.

Both ways are valuable, though it is only the former way that seems to find the light of day in contemporary schools. With Student Choice Curriculum, quite often teachers will be energetically engaged as co-discoverers in the student's work.

Similarly, the teacher-as-learner might wish to discover to what degree Lindsey can improvise and assimilate connections to the original situation, something educators recognize as an important component of cognitive development. The who-gets-the-money controversy might be linked to the way subsidies are provided by the US government to different people and businesses. Perhaps Lindsey can make some insightful connections about the fairness of each based on a critical juxtaposition suggested by her teacher. In a learner-learner paradigm, both parties have keen interests connecting them to the student's exploration.

When done well, Student Choice Curriculum keeps teachers actively engaged in ever-changing pedagogy to move their students toward flexible understanding and not just toward gathering knowledge. This is the magic of the learner-learner paradigm. Student Choice Curriculum will grow teacher skills in ways that traditional teaching does not. Her toolbox will adapt and grow and she will not only know the intended uses of each tool, but she will use each in diverse applications that call on myriad creative processes.

SHAPING STUDENT PRACTICE

Within the world of Student Choice Curriculum, because students' interests will be a measure of their learning, teachers will need to recruit and create authentic audiences of a diverse nature. Real people with real connections to the topics being studied have the potential to extend the challenge of learning beyond mere classroom work, forcing students to know in ways that demand internalized flexibility. Her teachers will not only have to learn how Lindsey's work demands its own authenticity within evaluative paradigms, they will also have to be savvy about who to bring in as observers of the student's work.

Some authentic audiences will be selected because of their current, practiced expertise while others will be selected due to their historic perspective. Depending upon the nature of the topic being explored, other criteria will be used. Thus, teachers will have to be knowledgeable and active within their communities to build the bridges between the school and those willing to help and support young learners.

For real learning to occur, students will need real-time opportunities to demonstrate and grow their skills. Those skills will often not be understood fully by a teacher who may have not particular experience in the student's topic of interest. As was suggested earlier, Lindsey may not find that all of her teachers have experience in or a love for the game of basketball.

But in the adult world of networking and community spirit, the teacher will serve as liaison between the student and the authentic audience that will assist in developing those skills. Moreover, the teacher will also serve as a gatekeeper so that when authentic audiences are contracted, the members of that audience will know their time will be well used.

Student Choice Curriculum will both encourage and direct teachers to become more committed to real-time, formative evaluation. Because of performance-based elements, teachers' work will occasionally take on qualities of a theatrical director, one who must use a critical eye each day as rehearsals continue, visualizing the way the individual actor uses the stage while simultaneously seeing the whole ensemble interacting.

There will be times when her teachers will have to step into the learning process and redirect Lindsey in order to focus her more directly on skills not yet internalized. At other times, though, the same kind of stimulus might be left untouched and then debriefed after the fact in an active learning reflection session. In this light, teachers will have to be savvy on the methods of real-time evaluative work and how each learner is affected by the process of redirection and reflection.

Moreover, Lindsey will be asked regularly to share her methods of exploration with other students, those who are undertaking both similar and divergent investigations. Within this context, the teacher will have to create different kinds of groups for different kinds of purposes, acknowledging that some meetings between students will need to be of homogeneous types—similar skill set or subject area or general topic of exploration—while other meetings will be heterogeneous—impromptu methods assessment or general process skills.

Group selection will bring together several teachers from several subject areas to discuss how their particular students are progressing in their studies. Such teacher meetings will be powerful integrators of curricular purpose, as they will bring together the science, the math, the English, the history, the art (including music), and the language teachers to discuss the many ways students will benefit from a cross-disciplinary meeting of minds.

The student meetings created by these brainstorming sessions will be instrumental for discovering how well those students are learning their chosen interest, seeing them juxtapose their own self-made theories with those of other students. For example, in one of these sessions Lindsey may see a link in both resources and justice comparing the who-gets-the-money controversy of collegiate athletics to the distribution of funds of the National Endowment of the Arts. Such a link demonstrates some essential meaning-making skills, and it is paramount to how Student Choice Curriculum will work.

In different contexts, students will need assistance developing projects, evaluations, and reflections, and these, too, will play a role in honing a teacher's tool kit. Lindsey may need a hand unpacking the next part of her exploration, another area where the teacher, by the nature of being a more mature learner, can be the "guide on the side" showing where the next junction or stopping point may be. Next steps can be hard for young learners, in part because they have been conditioned by our current system that the learning proceeds for a while and then stops to take a standardized test.

With Student Choice Curriculum, the paradigm will be that learning doesn't stop, though it may change direction or shape or function. A teacher's training in the processes of human learning and her experience at shaping units and yearlong studies will be the right skill set for keeping Lindsey's exploration fresh and forward moving. But as has been suggested, it will be an ever-changing skill set the teacher develops too.

Students will need encouragement. This should be the teacher's wheelhouse. But in Student Choice Curriculum, teachers, too, will need encouragement, and it will come not only from their colleagues but also from their students.

Imagine for a moment that Lindsey's teacher is not finding success in assembling the right authentic audience for her presentation on race and basketball. As the two meet to discuss this lack, it may be Lindsey who steps up to assure the teacher that things will be fine, that people will be found, and that all they—Lindsey and her teacher—have to do is keep plugging away at it. She'll probably volunteer to do some searching herself, since she is a local ballplayer and has been meeting many locals connected to basketball in a keen way. These learner-learner relationships will be wonderful opportunities for individuals to grow as colleagues-in-learning.

Students will, occasionally, need scolding. Teachers have done that for years. But in the context of Student Choice Curriculum, that scolding will be, in part, due to Lindsey not keeping up with her own plan, her own goals, her own desires.

Contemporary teachers scold their students for not reading all of *Great Expectations* or not doing all thirty-seven algebra problems for homework. But that work was assigned by the teacher and not necessarily embraced by the student. When Lindsey has selected her own area of interest and negotiated her own learning plan, responsibility lands on different shoulders. Lindsey becomes more than just a part of the learning process; she is the originator of that process.

Students will need attention, the right kind, the right amount, and at the right time. Well, that's life for anybody. In Student Choice Curriculum the attention will go both ways. No longer will the world of education be understood as a teacher-to-student paradigm. Student Choice Curriculum will be understood as a team-based process where more than one stakeholder is always involved in the action.

Top-down learning as the modus operandi has to stop. Even progressive-minded reformers who bemoan the conditions of the classroom, of the Common Core, and of the standardized testing movement often fail to move beyond these basics to what really matters: student learning. When students are not interested in the instruction, their level of engagement drops, they fail to internalize the learning, and very little of the classroom experience travels with them as they go from school to life.

They are then grossly underprepared to deal with the decisions and dilemmas they will face in creating their own lives. Once upon a time it may have been possible that students could graduate from high school with little sense of how to use their particular learning. Society's pace may have been such that adjacent generations could share the same knowledge back and forth, thus acculturating each other to the necessary standards of acceptable behavior, in the home and at work.

But that is no longer true. The world moves so quickly now that adjacent generations no longer share the same experiences. If we are not engaging students through the interests they bring to us, they will lose interest in the world we all share. That is a message of doom.

WHAT IT LOOKS LIKE—BEST PATH

Seeing and believing occupy spots on the same feedback loop: one can always lead to the other. Some readers are seeing how Student Choice Curriculum could work with a handful of students they know; but these readers may not be ready to believe in the system. Other readers may believe that allowing students more choice is an excellent way to restructure education; but these readers may not quite see how it will work clearly ... yet.

Imagine Lindsey as a ninth grader attending her first day of high school. She arrived on a bus and is waiting on the grounds with a few middle school friends. Signs and posters around the school announce the first meeting for first year students in the auditorium at 7:45 a.m., the starting time at this high school. Lindsey is excited about this first day, and when the bell announces the time to move to that meeting, she and her friends walk there gingerly.

Several teachers conduct the first meeting, along with many second- and third-year students who have firsthand experience with Student Choice Curriculum. Familiar music plays as the first-year students enter the auditorium, and each is handed an overview of the choices they will need to make in the next three weeks if they are to enroll in Student Choice Curriculum. A major point of the assembly is the desire for all students to take part in this program, but as it will put a lot of responsibility onto each of them, the decision should not be taken lightly.

To help in that decision, the meeting will detail several department meetings that will occur over the next five days to orient how the subject areas function in the development of each student's choice of study. Student presenters will share insights and take questions; community members who have been authentic audiences will present their role. This meeting is an orientation of what *must* happen—how, why, and by when—for each student to design her own educational program. Moreover, it will make clear what she needs to do when she becomes disoriented with the self-guided nature of these first three weeks.

Early requirements include creating a learning plan that describes the nature of the exploration for the first grading period. Lindsey, for example, will develop a plan that clarifies her intention to use basketball to pursue possible future employment as either a coach, a sports journalist, or a specialty support person for a basketball team or a program. This plan will help teachers structure the engagements and assessment that will frame her that first grading period.

Moreover, it will serve as a specific starting point for making the student responsible for her learning actions through all her time in Student Choice Curriculum. This initial plan is absolutely flexible and adaptable, but without having formed one in those first three weeks, the student will be enrolled in the school's traditional curriculum.

Other meetings in the first three weeks will be similar to this first meeting, though delivered in academic departments. Each subject area will hold orientation meetings for all students, the new and returning, clarifying issues and procedures. New staff will be entering schools on a regular basis, and students need to be privy to the skills and areas of interest these people bring.

As schools, over time, become more comfortable with Student Choice Curriculum, new tools and tactics will be developed and implemented.

Orientation meetings will introduce these as well. Mostly, though, these meetings will inform students of how and when learning opportunities will be presented by the departments.

Specific classes on necessary skills will be offered regularly; studio work for students focused on skills that connect to their topic of interest will be available; and as has been suggested, there will be interactive meetings where students meet with others who are working in the subject area though, perhaps, in different topics of exploration. Department orientations will be given three times (per subject area) in the first eight days of school so all students can attend one for each subject area. The very new are encouraged, and sometimes choose, to repeat some meetings.

Another requirement will be grade-level meetings to be attended by the administrative staff, the counseling team, the students, and at least one parent or guardian for each student. Student Choice Curriculum shifts significant responsibility to the students to self-motivate and self-evaluate, so a clear sense of those lines of responsibility must be drawn. For example, normal graduation requirements will be discontinued in Student Choice Curriculum, and it will be possible for some students to matriculate away from the school in three years, maybe less.

When teachers, administrators, and authentic audiences feel a student has attained sought-after skills, and that those skills show the student to be ready for the next step in her education, she should be allowed to graduate and move on to that next level of learning. This means many students will not need four years to complete high school but could find themselves seeking college admission or work much earlier. Any current high school teacher knows many students for whom the final year (or more) has not been an effective use of their academic time.

The reverse of this is also true: many students may not develop their skills effectively and not internalize their own self-created learning program. Thus it may be necessary for a student to be moved back into the traditional curricular structure in order to graduate. Or a student might need an extra year to demonstrate the particular and general skills for completing Student Choice Curriculum. This could play havoc with the normal concept of high school as a four-year process, but that's not a bad thing. Everyone should question how the idea of a four-year plan got put into practice.

Parents, however, will need to know this from the very beginning of Student Choice Curriculum. Administrators and counselors will need to clarify significant details; students will need to understand how this special opportunity may change drastically from what they have imagined high school to be. Indeed, it could happen that a student is involved in Student Choice Curriculum in one year but not the next (as in Anthony's case, described earlier). As it always happens, changing responsibility alters outcomes.

Consequently, these meetings will need to be held annually for each student, so to keep the transparency of the program's goals and conditions clear to all. Failure to attend these meetings will always result in being returned to the traditional curriculum.

One other element of Student Choice Curriculum is the option for each newly entered student to have a "buddy" who is already matriculating in the program. As often as possible, this should be a one-on-one student relationship, but it could just as easily and effectively be a one-on-three with the three being the newcomers if the one older student were truly an effective communicator and nurturer. Students will sign up for buddies and meet those who might buddy them in a social event in those first eight days.

WHAT IT LOOKS LIKE—LESSER PATH

It must also be possible that some students might move into Student Choice Curriculum having missed the three-week deadline. For sure, many students will be unready to do the necessary work of those initial eight days, much as they may try. But hearing from friends or watching others move through the program, they may want to take part, and this should be possible: students should not have to wait for next year to enroll.

By virtue of working within the traditional curriculum, these students will interact with classroom teachers on a daily basis. Thus their skill sets will be known, and they can petition those teachers for the chance to move into Student Choice Curriculum based on those skills. Different schools will see this differently, but there is logic in the idea that having missed the eight-day deadline, a student wanting to transition in will need permission from all teachers on her learning team. If everyone except her math teacher feels she'd be fine in Student Choice Curriculum, it won't be enough.

Of course, in her second year, she'll have the same start-of-school, eight-day orientation, so she could step into the program then. Every student at the school, if they meet the eight-day deadlines, can become a part of Student Choice Curriculum in any year. It then remains their job to prove they can stay.

A PRACTICE RUN

Student Choice Curriculum will work by putting the student at the center of planning and processing of her learning. Teachers will operate, most of the time, by asking themselves, "what does this student need?" Some may argue this is always a teacher's central question, and that should be right. But it's not how education plays out in today's schools. Too often the demand is only for the nature of the subject, with the question being, "what do these kids need to know about algebra?"

With this change of focus, along with the learner-learner relationships defined earlier, teachers and students will work together to build skills needed to achieve the goals the student has set for herself. Undoubtedly teachers will have significant input on many aspects of the learning, but it will also be true that students, from time to time, will hold the upper hand.

Unfortunately this kind of change may be an obstacle toward implementation, as schools may not know how to operate with students setting the agenda for their own goals. Thus, it is important to see how Student Choice Curriculum could be practiced in a working school. Many avenues exist for its entry into a school, but this one seems the most reasonable for current staff and administrative teams.

Begin with thirty-five to forty students, handpicked, representing multiple grade and ability levels—nine to ten students for each grade level. Handpicking is important because there's a significant number of students in every high school who present themselves in such a way that their teachers know them to be flexible and willing to take risks. These students, who might include the valedictorian or the last member of the class, possess an understanding of life, and they know how to work in the real world with real people. Whether they move onto college or not, these students have demonstrated to their teachers that they will be all right in what they do.

Make sure students are evenly distributed across your program. If equity across the years is difficult to establish, be bottom heavy: have more ninth graders than tenth, eleventh, and twelfth, in that order. That way when you meet with success, you won't lose too many through initial graduation.

Select some bright students who work toward best efforts, some average students who present a range of work ethics, and those who find it hard to be motivated by what school offers. If you can, include socioeconomics in your selection, again by varying broadly across that spectrum.

Yes, as far as experiments go, random sampling would be better than handpicked. Yes, in order to juxtapose data, control groups engender deeper understanding. But for the purpose of seeing how this program would work, don't fret the experimental nature at this point. Select your pool of students and get started.

The next step is to get those students to sit with at least one administrator to select the teachers who will work with them to make Student Choice Curriculum happen. This is a very important step, for you want to have teachers who can create the learner-learner relationships that are so important for this educational paradigm. The students you select will know best who those teachers will be. The administrator's role is to be sure the students are fair and complete, and that all of them take part in the process of determining who will be selected. The administrator should not have voting rights in the decision.

You will need one teacher in each department of math, history, English, and art; and you might need two in the foreign languages and the sciences, depending on the thirty-five students in your program. While some of the students will be involved in physical education, you might get by with just a brief training for that teacher, but there's no reason not to include one from that department. A psychology teacher could help as well.

Once the students and teachers are selected, put all of them in a room, including the students' parents, and set some guidelines. Clarify your goals and purposes and the elements of Student Choice Curriculum: the topic of interest, the authentic audiences, the changed nature of the daily schedule, the student's responsibility in the learning paradigm, and the multiple venues of learning. Describe how the interactions with the teachers will occur, where the student's and the teacher's responsibility intersect, and where that responsibility separates.

Let them know that they'll be asked to do a lot next year (yes, you will need to have this meeting in the spring before starting, which makes including the ninth-grade group difficult). They will work in ways they have not been asked to work before. Let them know that *in every possible way* the school will stand with them and help them through all obstacles and that there will be no crises that cannot be conquered.

In other words, you must promise that regardless of what happens academically, nothing will affect their status as a student in your school. Provided they treat the program with dignity and effort, they will maintain their grade-point average (GPA); they will earn the credits for graduation for the classes they are enrolled in; they will take part in all school functions. The risk for this first group is all on the school, not on the students. Bring them to agreement and allow them and their parents to sign a contract communicating the goals and plans. Then get the ball moving.

Teachers, obviously, are a big part of this experiment, though it is hard to clarify just who will be the ones to take to the job most readily. That's a prime reason for letting the students play such a significant role in their selection. Moreover, as an initial foundation for the appropriateness of the program, by allowing the students to select the teachers they will be sharing that experience with, you assure their buy-in to the program, which may allow you a bargaining chip if needed later.

You want positive people involved in this experiment. Students know the positive teachers, the ones who make connections with their learners and who make learning fun. Giving students this kind of respect will go a long way to help get your program started.

You will need at least one administrator who serves as the Student Choice Curriculum liaison, especially in the first three weeks of the year, when the students go through the process of making their selection, negotiating with teachers, and planning out their year. As the year progresses, this person will meet with students, parents, and teachers to explore and evaluate the program. This person cannot be someone who believes the traditional way of education is the best.

Throughout the year there must be plenty of meetings, reassessments, and new plans of action. Each of the meetings should include as many stakeholders as possible, including parents. It is important to remember that with Student Choice Curriculum the students' choices matter, so as you are practicing this program in your school, students need to be a major part of the evaluation process.

Moreover, the practice will reveal which of the teachers fit the character traits that serve this program well; it will also help demonstrate the specific traits that might not have been considered in early planning sessions. The first year will show good and bad ways to recruit and organize authentic audiences, to assemble students in the Collaborative Work Spaces or the Social Hall, and to evaluate students' fit in the program.

There are myriad elements to Student Choice Curriculum that cannot be imagined right now, mainly because it is such a major paradigm change. Your school's practice will allow the growth and detailed data that will translate the process from idea to reality.

IMAGINING OTHER LEVELS

As has been presented here, Student Choice Curriculum is a high school program, though its scope and function should not be limited to that venue. All grade levels could incorporate Student Choice Curriculum, following Jerome Bruner's idea that anything that can be learned or taught can be learned or taught at any level, so long as the approach is adapted properly to the learner's skill set and intellectual zone of proximal development. Bruner was focused on topics of instruction more than pedagogy, but that doesn't mean his insight is not fitting for this kind of curricular change.

Student Choice Curriculum might work very well in the elementary or middle school years, though it would take teachers of those grade levels to design and incorporate the intricacies necessary, just as it will be the teachers of a high school who do the same there. However, as readers were allowed to look somewhat closely at the meetings and responsibilities of the first two weeks of high school, they can gain some insights of the same time period for a first grade incorporating Student Choice Curriculum.

The only difference will be that this description will be more narrative in its approach. Imagine day one of first grade, in a small school that has been using Student Choice Curriculum for a few years. Excited students meet excited teachers; it could look like this:

Desks, tables, chairs, bookcases, books, framed and unframed artwork, and sundry classroom materials are stacked somewhat haphazardly in a gymnasium. File cabinets stand near plastic blue chairs, but those same chairs—ones looking just like them—stand along another wall beside cans of yardsticks and brooms and squeegees.

Looking closely at the collection, one might, if she had spent some time in elementary schools over the years, see in the arrangement some sort of order or pattern, but that would take a special eye. Most everyone else would not see rhyme nor reason to the gathering of goods in that gym. Three janitors talk beside hand trucks and wagons, ready, it seems, to move this equipment to the classrooms where it belongs.

And why not? It is the first day of school at Chapleton Elementary, and for a short while now, students have been assembling in the hallways and cafeteria, some talking quietly with friends, some standing with their parents, and some standing by themselves, ready for another year of school.

Signs with teachers' names and room numbers have been taped onto lockers throughout the small school; similar signs have been taped to classroom doors. Mrs. Jackson, Room 212, catches our eye and, because the door is held open by a wooden wedge with the label 212, we look inside. The floor is glossy from a fresh waxing; the white boards gleam; the window curtains are pulled back, and daylight streams in. The walls are bare, and a smell of fresh paint permeates the vicinity.

Mrs. Jackson comes from the back closet having just hung up her raincoat—it may shower this afternoon. She walks to the whiteboard and plucks a marker from the tray. She hesitates, remembering when she was a student, days of chalkboards and neat little rows of open-topped desks. She smiles and writes her name on the board in bold, cursive script, and she awaits her collection of new first graders, all twenty-two of them.

At the sound of an announcement on the intercom the children begin to move toward their classrooms. Some are in their third and last year at Chapelton, and these children escort and guide newer students toward their rooms. They are wearing Chapelton green, as their mascot is the Clover, and they each have a four-leaf emblem on their shirts. Some of the children are still with their parents, or parent, and, of course, some are with older sisters or brothers.

Most of the teachers, including Mrs. Jackson, have stepped to their doors to welcome the children to their class. Mrs. Jackson has taught at Chapelton for many years, long enough to remember when first days meant having each desk labeled, ready, and waiting for each student, when rules and schedules were preset and names were called in alphabetical order on a daily basis to see who was present and absent.

She remembers having determined a seating chart before the children arrived, predicting who should sit by whom based on siblings or intuition or other teacher input. Sometimes she got it right. In those days the teacher created the first bulletin boards and determined the artwork on the walls. Students came to a prefabricated room that presented a welcoming attitude toward learning. Mrs. Jackson liked those years, liked how it allowed her to show her students just who their teacher was on day one.

But she also likes this new way. She likes how everything truly starts fresh. She likes that the students will begin their learning experiences by making decisions: will they have tables or desks in their classroom? How will they organize those? Rows? Groups? Shapes? Will they want matching colors for their chairs? Where should the teacher's desk go? How will they get these things from the gymnasium to the classroom?

All of these decisions are necessary for this classroom to become a place of learning. What Mrs. Jackson likes most about this new way is that now it is her job to help her students make their room a place of learning; and if they do it well, her students will know it is their place of learning.

Mrs. Jackson knows she must be watching all of her students on day one quite closely. She knows that some will be natural leaders while others will be naturally shy. She knows both types populate all learning environments, both types populate all human spaces, and she knows both types are capable of making good decisions.

Her job on day one is to recognize and maneuver the blend of personalities so that the children collaborate to create their space. Some will know the importance of action; others will know the importance of patience; some will be demanding while others will be sensitive; each characteristic wrought properly from the individual can influence the process positively.

Mrs. Jackson knows it is not easy, these days of getting the school year started, and just as it was years ago, she might get some of it wrong. But in this new world of Student Choice Curriculum, Mrs. Jackson likes the real-time feel of the experience. It is not as much getting it right or wrong as it is a guidance of possibilities, a framing of futures. One thing she is pretty sure of is that this year's class, in personality, in priority, in special determinants, will be nothing like last year's.

This is another thing she likes a great deal.

"Children," she encourages her class. "We've got to get some things for our room so we can begin this year of learning. We're going to be together in this room until June, and we've got the challenge of deciding how to make

it our own." She pauses and looks around, checking for those who have both eyes on her, for those who have both eyes out the window, and for those who have both eyes on the floor. "In the gymnasium there are all sorts of things we might be able to use in here, but we have to decide what those things will be. Who can tell me, by raising your hand, what this classroom needs right now?"

Nearly all hands shoot toward the ceiling. These first graders have learned some of the practices of school in their earlier educational experiences. Mrs. Jackson needs only to tap into their prior knowledge to get the ball rolling. First graders already know about desks and tables, and most have had opportunities to experience both in different preschool or kindergarten classrooms. They've sat on floors and chairs, on stools and hassocks. They have a sense of the classroom, but making it their own, furnishing it themselves . . . those are new things.

She takes a few suggestions from several students, trying hard to get them to clarify their choice, while also trying to get input from each of the out-the-window, right-at-her, and on-the-floor set of eyes. As decisions are being made, she checks these with the students. "I'm hearing that many of you want tables rather than desks. Does this sound like the right way to have our classroom look?" And she makes sure to address one or two of those who don't seem to be self-starters.

To some degree, she'll shape the possibilities for some of those kids, seeking their input by letting them know, "We could have both tables and desks if that sounds like a good idea. What do you think?" Everything about this first day, and, ultimately, this first week needs to demonstrate to the students that it will be their thoughts, their ability to envision and to share those visions with each other that will make this classroom their personal learning space. These are simple decisions for teachers to make, and so for years teachers have made them before the kids arrive. But in Student Choice Curriculum, the shifting of decisions to the students is central to all learning tasks, even on day one in first grade.

Student Choice Curriculum recognizes that decision-making promotes a different kind of thoughtfulness than traditional schools have offered. At Chapleton, first graders will be exposed to a very new and dynamic process as they furnish their classroom in those first few days. Their teacher will motivate and maneuver her students so they can make decisions through a consistent interaction with all the minds there.

She will balance the decision-making across the spectrum of personal characteristics that populate her students. Considering that each of these students will have spent time already in a variety of classrooms, it is fair to imagine they know how some kids will have different characteristics than they do. Their teacher will work that diversity to an advantage just as good office *managers, good life coaches, and good spouses recognize how strengths come in differences.*

As the week moves forward, students will be asked to determine other elements of their year together. How and when will they leave their classroom for physical education, for visits to the media center? What parts of their room will be used for quiet study and which for group work? What kind of learning centers will be featured in their classroom? How long will they be available? Who will be responsible for taking care of them?

Many of these questions will be ongoing, continually visited choices during the year. Students should learn, in this first year, that learning is something they shape with their own influence, and that if they share their influence, they will find outcomes to be more conducive to what everyone wants.

Mrs. Jackson likes that her students look around the room with opened mouths. When she mentions they have to bring the desks (or tables, or both) into the room and asks, "who wants to help with that?" nearly all hands go up. She thanks them for being such good students and simultaneously challenges them: "And where will we put these desks? How do you want them arranged? Who will sit by whom?"

What Mrs. Jackson really likes is that learning has become something tied to real-time decisions learners make about the environment in which they work. No longer will an outsider or adult tell them how the room will be, or when reading, writing, or arithmetic will occur; now the students will decide about those processes of their learning.

Moreover, the new process allows Mrs. Jackson to extend the welcome and encourage her students to bring things from home in order to make their classroom more familiar, more friendly, more like a place of comfort and control. As her students consider how desks might be arranged, she can encourage them to think about other things that might make the room a better place. Two years ago, one of her first graders thought a rug might be nice because he loved to lie on one in front of the fireplace at his home and play with his cat.

Not everyone agreed with this student, but it was decided that a part of the room could have the rug, and kids could use it when they wanted. Teachers have always helped students navigate these moments of potential conflict without resolving it for them. It is a matter of making decisions, making choices in the context of being a part of a larger social group. Student Choice Curriculum brings this practice to the forefront of the learning process.

Some of the teachers found the first days more contentious because of this room-setting process. Without question, it is hard for first graders to conceptualize a place where learning should occur; their experience as classroom learners is short-lived. In some classrooms, students' decisions for how desks would be arranged were often non-efficacious, which made it difficult for the teacher to see how she would teach.

Moreover, the process could be fraught with problems of personal interactions. Some students were bossy; some were diffident; some made fast decisions while others needed more time and found themselves following others rather than being allowed to make decisions. Many teachers, due to their own personalities, found this to be difficult to manage, especially as it was contrary to how they were educated themselves.

But isn't that life all over, Mrs. Jackson thought to herself. Aren't all of us differently skilled in the decision-making processes that become our lives? Shouldn't we invite young learners into the process of practicing those skills and then offer them chances to reflect upon those skills? While she knew that first grade was not necessarily the time to dive headfirst into philosophy, it made sense to her that even a five- or six-year-old could wrap her head around the idea that the unexamined life might not be as fun as the examined one.

Mrs. Jackson also felt that while one set of decisions were being made about the desks, if she were clever enough, she might also prepare the kids for another set of decisions about snack time or lunch or when they might go to the media center. She knew that as the year progressed, her job would include making sure that each and every child spent "quality time" with each and every other child to share, in pairs, in trios, and in small groups, the nature of their special interest of study. Getting them together on this first day so they could get a feel for each other and begin to learn the qualities that made working relationships function was important.

As the kids came into her room, one by one, or in small groups who might already be friends, she was watching, watching their eyes and their smiles, watching the ways they sat comfortably (on the floor for now) beside someone or closer to another, or if they separated themselves from the group at large. All of this information Mrs. Jackson was collecting was important. She observed and sifted through her years of experience, so that when she started her students thinking about their first task, she might know better how to watch them.

"Good morning, children," she began with a positive emphasis only a first grade teacher can muster. "I am delighted to see you all today, your first day of first grade." She was walking among them, around them, stepping over their legs and occasionally touching a shoulder or the top of a head. She was getting their attention. All eyes were on her. And then she stopped. "Who is going to help us get those desks inside our classroom?"

Nearly every hand shot toward the ceiling.

DOUBLING DOWN ON THE MAJOR ISSUES

1. The metaphor of seeking a guru works well for education, as it draws on the way personal interest motivates learners to seek new skills.
2. Contemporary learning paradigms fail to dignify student interest and thereby negate the role that interest plays in coordinating intellectual growth and critical thought; students become disinterested in the lessons of education and in the world we share.
3. Education must derive from the bottom up, in a process shared by teacher and student, so that students do not miss significant opportunities to connect their learning to the particular issues that mark their lives.
4. Student Choice Curriculum dignifies the learner by shaping student learning based on goals and terms negotiated by the student (and teacher).
5. Focusing on the interests of the student will: (1) create paradigms that more effectively develop minds attuned to problem-finding; and (2) shift the responsibility for what needs to be learned more directly to the student.
6. Because the most significant relationship in education is learner-learner, not teacher-student, Student Choice Curriculum recognizes teachers as occasional co-discoverers in the students' exploration.
7. Student Choice Curriculum will reengage teachers in the learning process by centralizing their work around the question, "What does this student need right now?" This will grow new skills of human understanding for the teacher.
8. Student Choice Curriculum is potentially sound for all grade levels. Anything that can be learned can be learned at any level. Only the approach much be adapted to the proper fit for the learners.
9. Current understanding misconstrues choice as an economic and not a learning issue.

Chapter 5

The Learning Environments

The greatest sign of success for a teacher is to be able to say, the children are now working as if I did not exist.

—Montessori

FRAMING THOUGHTS

Sometimes it is important to remember that where things happen matters a great deal. Most of us are more at ease in our backyard than we are at the grocery store. Most of us prefer to be beside a pool waiting for a cool drink than in a waiting room preparing for a doctor's visit. Yet many of us have experienced waiting rooms and grocery stores that please us and make the experience of being there better. Education should be no different. As you explore the ideas in this chapter, wrap your minds around the potential for changing the physical spaces of schools. Ponder the relationship between learning spaces and learning outcomes, and let yourself imagine how different spaces will help create different learners. Moreover, remember those things of your own high school that you know needed changing, and bring those thoughts to the paragraphs of this chapter.

Because most high schools have not been designed with Student Choice Curriculum in mind, significant changes in both the physical plant and the teachers' paradigm of learning spaces will have to be made. If the world were perfect there would be money available to retrofit the old as well as to build new schools throughout the land. In that fantasy, schools could be designed from the ground up to facilitate the more interactive environment Student Choice Curriculum would create.

These schools would incorporate the open spaces of contemporary office buildings and hospitals, spaces that invite diverse mental work, especially creativity. There would be common areas where people can meet to share ideas and to discuss, debate, and detail plans and practices. But this kind of change will not occur any time soon. Thus, Student Choice Curriculum will have to find ways to fit into the already improper environments that describe most American schools. This chapter will describe some of that refitting.

A visit to most high schools in the United States would reveal learning spaces that are outdated, both in their function and their form. Schools look decades old even when they are newly built, and older ones often have portable classrooms taking up what was once green space around the school.

The condition of our schools is a major problem for education, which must be dealt with even if Student Choice Curriculum is never embraced. Contemporary learning spaces are not friendly, and little is being done to change that. If Student Choice Curriculum is implemented, it will almost surely be in existing schools, and the changes therein will have to be retrofitted and jerry-rigged to a significant degree.

CHANGING THE LEARNING SPACES

It is important to note that changes will need to be more than bricks and mortar, more than alterations to the physical space. Just as important will be the development of new attitudes about the spaces where learning occurs. Student Choice Curriculum seeks to alter paradigms, so even if the building cannot be significantly restructured, the metaphorical feel of the schools will need to be distinctively different. Think form and function.

Because the school day will function differently, the learning spaces will need to be reimagined, even personified, as agents for shaping those different functions. Because more educational interactions will be student-to-student, the spaces will need to be designed to invite thoughtful work, not just high school gossip.

The school itself will need to speak a visual and structural language of respect, for both students and the ideas they will develop and share. Teachers know how a change of environment can alter the mindfulness of a group of students. A simple class trip to the media center often demonstrates this clearly. Moreover, quality instruction can motivate students to work well in small groups and to develop excellent products when they are allowed to learn socially.

The spaces of this school will need to speak a varying architectural language to the students who occupy them, encouraging that feeling of being in a new learning space. While this book has argued that it is the students' personal interests that motivate significant learning, the spaces, too, help in the motivation process. When the right spaces cause the proper intellectual investment, students will more readily do the work of their own design.

Imagine these spaces as inviting, comfortable, and spacious places people enjoy. All of us have been in rooms that inspire us; all of us have been in spaces that make us want to leave immediately. Learning environments need to be designed with students in mind; they need to be places where students want to be. They have to be designed so students not only see where learning derives, but also where life intersects.

The Cafeteria and Auditorium

The cafeteria needs to be a place where anyone would like to eat, regularly. Moreover, it should be a place where many nonstudents do eat daily. Certainly some students in Student Choice Curriculum will choose the culinary arts or restaurant management as their topics of exploration (David, described earlier, fits this profile), and they should be given opportunities to create their own culinary delights and front-of-the-house practices for real people looking for a good lunch.

When you think of the cafeteria, think of how theme parks like Walt Disney World's Epcot have created dining halls for the fare of each country. Or imagine art and science museums that have crafted thematic dining spaces so while you grab your lunch, you are still within the collection or artifacts. If you need a smaller scale idea, think of how fast-food chain Chipotle has made their dining rooms comfortable and casual. High school cafeterias are generally chaotic. That must change.

Most auditoriums need to be updated, with modernized seating that would allow a comfortable sitting through *Long Day's Journey into Night* without an intermission. Auditoriums should be able to show a major motion picture or host a jazz ensemble or a TEDx function, both acoustically and technically. These spaces need to be flexible as well as functional. Given that drama programs in non-performance arts high schools often have small enrollments, this space needs to facilitate simultaneous multiuse.

Here will be where local political meetings will be held. Here will be the stage for the teacher debates mentioned earlier. There are always possibilities for touring theatrical groups to be hired by a school. The auditorium in a Student Choice Curriculum school should get a great deal of use during school and after hours.

Later in this chapter, when specific spaces are described, you should consider how some of those might work well inside the auditorium. Understanding that most schools are unable to create new, ornate spaces of learning, repurposing available spaces will be the best way to solve these issues. An auditorium is large enough to house many people at one time, and it could be fairly easily sectioned into three or four useable spaces.

Of course, because some students will have chosen the performing arts or event planning as their topic of exploration, much of the functional organization for events in the auditorium can be handled by the students. Indeed, this is part of the attitude change within Student Choice Curriculum: students are "in charge." In truth, it is a shared oversight, but as students will be studying their interests, it is fair to assume that some will want to be theater or event managers one day, so working out logistical details for the auditorium will be a good task for them to manage.

The Classrooms

Classrooms, too, will need to be rethought. Many will no longer be classrooms as regularly understood, but rather repurposed into more of a seminar or study center, a place where students can come and go more openly, retrieve and share information they need, and then comfortably work on skill sets in groups or by themselves. It makes sense that many classrooms will be designed as suites with connecting passages so that differentiated needs can be met in adjoining spaces.

Direct instruction will still occur at a Student Choice Curriculum school, both for the students enrolled in that program and the others who have remained in the traditional curriculum. But even in the rooms that perform the lion's share of direct instruction, the practice in the classroom needs to be differentiated into a less institutionalized, more alluring space of choice and opportunity. Thus what's on the walls, and what's used for lighting, and how the desks and tables are aligned needs to be conceptualized differently.

In this frame of thinking, a suite of rooms in the English department where issues of journalistic writing are presented will be important for Lindsey's choice of basketball; she may find herself there quite often. Indeed, writing might be a significant element in most topics of interest, especially as students may see their interest as a way to make a living. Strong writers generally seem able to find work in our culture, so focusing on different elements of the written world will be an important part of Student Choice Curriculum.

For this journalistic space, imagine a three-room suite of adjoining classrooms. Perhaps it is an L-shaped suite or maybe it's aligned linearly. Lindsey will come to know this space well, for she will use one room to get some direct instruction on the nature of journalistic writing, the creation of leads, the top-loading of the story, and the right way to attribute known and "off the record" quotations. Another room will be where she does the work of journalism, the processing of research, the drafting of the story, or the final revision for submission.

The third room would be more of a meeting place, where students interact with each other, sharing information and problems and comparing skill-set developments. Obviously all three rooms would be staffed with teachers, and part of the process of using the room will come through appointments and adapted schedules, though drop-ins will not be denied. The point is that the school will be divided up differently into different kinds of spaces, to enhance a flexible and more responsive relationship with the immediate and long-range needs of the students.

Each subject area will have spaces like this journalism "wing," though each may find that different student demands create different needs. One learning center in the language "wing" may include all the necessary resources for every foreign language taught at the school. One history center might be dedicated just to the use of particular databases. Each Student Choice Curriculum school will need to tap into the strengths of its teachers as it also navigates the needs of its students and their interests.

The Campus

It will also be important that the school has some green spaces where students can visit to study or to relax. It should be expected that some students will want to explore landscape design, or botany, or agriculture, or heirloom vegetables as their chosen topic, so there must be places where they can learn and apply those skills. Greenhouses, perhaps, and gardens of flowers and vegetables would be necessary spaces for student learning. They would also be good ways for students to become involved in the very human activity of growing food.

Students involved in these kinds of study will obviously take the time to be in those spaces, observing and caring for plants, keeping walkways clear of debris, and generally interacting with their focal area in topic-specific ways. But these spaces should also be where students, if proper arrangements have been made, unwind and relax in a somewhat natural environment. It should never be forgotten that schools can be stressful places, and that humans often find natural spaces to release stress. Designing a school with all of this in mind would be a positive move toward a better future for education.

Suffice it to say, despite efforts to update physical spaces and to emphasize safety and acceptance, most schools do not meet this kind of aesthetic or functional criteria. Indeed, it seems as if schools are designed for the sole purpose of moving kids from one wing to another, one floor to another, one building to another, at a set of given times, in a method that can only be described as herding.

Between four to seven times per day, schools move great numbers of students, then deposit them in a classroom for the next forty-five or ninety minutes depending on the school's scheduling paradigm. We move 2,500 students seven times every day where I work. John A. Ferguson High School in Miami, Florida, moves 4,200 students daily.

Student Choice Curriculum will not move that many students at any one time. Such practice is anathema to education. Part of the conversation this book seeks should consider school traffic from space to space as more individually determined. Students will still need to be in the right place at the right time, and events like breakfasts, lunches, and assemblies will still need to function smoothly. However, Student Choice Curriculum's focus on the individual's selected topic of interest will open up a very different kind of practice inside the school, and no longer will one bell evoke the Pavlovian movement to the next class.

Also within the context of school design, teams will have to consider spaces that are often thought of as outside of the learning process, but still essential to the quality of learning: bathrooms, halls (width and length), counseling centers, and even entry and exit spaces for moving in and out of the school.

Some of these are nearly impossible to retrofit—hallways cannot easily be changed in most schools without major reconstruction, but when possible, student traffic could be redirected or limited to one way so that the feel of the hall changes. Artwork could be added; walls could be repainted so that all halls were a different color. Students should move about a school with little stress or congestion; there should not be a western round-up feel when large numbers of students travel from one part of the school to another.

But with other spaces, more flexibility can occur as updates in these spaces are often annual concerns. For example, the bathroom situation at every school ought to be modernized, and everything about them should be clean and well cared for daily. It should never be a thought in any students' mind that they will not go to the bathroom because of its condition.

Without exception, every student should have a locked space for personal items, and every learning area should have a system for storing student "stuff," so that when a learner arrives at a learning environment, she knows where to put her things safely and with confidence. Where possible, access to the outdoors should be a part of all classrooms. If we want our young learners to be energized by learning, we must make their space more inviting.

Schools need to become more of the kind of place where feel-good attitudes are grown. Indeed, it may be the attitude that is the most important part of this learning paradigm. Allowing students to choose their learning plan places new emphasis on them in the learning process. Making the spaces of the school fit that emphasis will help nurture the process into success. As has been suggested throughout, each school will go about this differently, that's why a conversation about Student Choice Curriculum needs to begin.

THE UNIQUE PLACES OF STUDENT CHOICE CURRICULUM

By the time students get to high school, they have more adult-type needs regarding their learning relationships. As Student Choice Curriculum allows students to invest personal time and energy into their own interests and aptitudes, they will find an increased need to: (1) socially interact with individual and group interests; and (2) spend significant time alone in reflective intellectual exploration. The learning spaces that follow will be designed to accomplish both of those tasks.

Moreover, the ways students will access these spaces—the number of visits, the time spent there, and the fellow students encountered—will be a part of the monitoring system of Student Choice Curriculum. Learners need a certain amount of practice to develop expertise in any skill area, a time often construed as ten thousand hours. Thus, the kind of time students spend here will matter.

In other words, it will not be possible for Lindsey to move forward in her educational exploration—or to graduate—without having set and met specific requirements in each of these learning spaces. This is one of the nonnegotiable elements of Student Choice Curriculum. Time on task will be spent in each of the learning centers. And students will be held responsible for demonstrating how their time was spent. This is true for all learning spaces. A brief description of each follows.

The Social Hall

When you imagine the Social Hall, think of a coffee shop or reading room, with comfortable furniture, good panoramic windows, and lots of books and magazines. The space should invite mingling. Certainly it would be Wi-Fi equipped with audiovisual equipment, but this is not a game room, nor is it a place that promotes multitasking. Students will attend the Social Hall to read and do necessary work, and they may find themselves engaged in conversations about their topics and progress with other students doing similar work. But these two activities should be separate from each other.

The Social Hall—and all Student Choice Curriculum learning centers—will be supervised not only to keep the focus on intellectual pursuits but also to assist students in the time-management skills young learners so often need. Acknowledging that growing minds benefit from shared interactions with others who have, due to life experiences, already participated in the construction of knowledge recognizes that such conversations must have a place in schools. But recognizing that such conversations can draw learners away from particular and important tasks of the moment is also a significant skill that needs to be developed.

The Social Hall will be a place where students will gather, in part because it may feel less like learning and more like play. But if the school staffs this learning space properly, students will discern in short notice that the Social Hall is a focused part of their learning. A goal of Student Choice Curriculum is to teach students how to learn, so it will be important for them to explore that aspect of the learning in different learning environments.

Lindsey will need to develop methods of sharing ideas with others to get a sense of how her progress matches theirs or how she might develop a new solution to a problem she's encountered—something like think/pair/share on steroids. But there will also be times when she needs to focus significantly on the task at hand even as others share and discuss. The Social Hall can be both of those places and it can be a place where the former grows into the latter.

Student Choice Curriculum will work hard to demonstrate the broad range of behaviors that make up significant learning. No one will graduate from Student Choice Curriculum who has not spent significant time in these learning spaces, and who has not, for each space, received an assessment of her work there. Part of that assessment will include reflective journals that record the moments spent in each place.

Some schools may create the Social Hall as a place where students can watch certain television or similar media, provided these fit in with general applications of projects being completed or if they fulfill a significant need to stay in touch with a major event of the social realm. For example, in an election season, it would not be wrong to expect that students could watch speeches, debates, or other commentary on the nature of electoral issues. This is a choice the school would make, depending on many factors, including numbers of students and limitations of physical space.

As mentioned, students will be monitored for the amount of time they spend in the Social Hall as well as for how they spend that time. Such time could be portioned out based on other aspects of the curriculum, something like a reward, though not merely as that. There are times when every student needs the creative ambience of a coffee shop just to be with friends and share life. Students at school should not be deprived of these experiences. If done right, with the right space and supervision, such experiences could be modeled there.

The Quiet Chambers

When you think of the Quiet Chambers, think of a small office with a desk and comfortable chair, a bookcase, and some very good lighting. A computer and printer should be available, and the room would be adorned in colors that contradict the institutional setting schools generally manifest.

The work here will be the highly focused work of finishing a paper or preparing the notes for an oral presentation or, for some students, the reading of a significant text. Students who discover their own learning styles and habits will come to know that some of their learning needs benefit from solitude. Sometimes you must just lock yourself into your room and work. That's what the Quiet Chambers will accomplish.

While the Quiet Chamber will be equally valuable with all other learning spaces, it may be difficult for many schools to create this space for every student. However, most high schools have been tasked to create similar spaces for students to take computer-based tests, and they have solved this problem by creating many cubicles housing a single computer keyboard, a mouse, and a monitor. Consequently, schools can create small spaces when needed. If they created similar single-testing cubicles and allowed each to serve five or six students—friends—they would accomplish the Quiet Chamber need.

Moreover, if the Quiet Chamber had to be shared, students could experience the different focus-patterns humans have, perhaps learning new ways to adjust their own learning schedules along the way. Just as all students will need time in the Social Hall—some will flourish there—some will need time to flourish in the Quiet Chambers. Thus, it will be mandatory that students not only do some significant work there but that they also show what kind of work they produced in that same reflective journal already mentioned.

As with all learning spaces, the Quiet Chambers will be monitored, but in a very different way. It makes little sense to place a teacher in the chamber, as that defeats the purpose of singular study. Perhaps a sign-up sheet will be used, coupled with a checklist of work done per session. Thus, Lindsey will check into the Quiet Chamber on Tuesday at 10:00 a.m. and check out at 11:00. She'll need to see the monitor when she arrives and leaves, showing the nature of work accomplished.

The work will be part of Lindsey's demonstration of particular skills completed in the Quiet Chambers, and the monitoring teacher will evaluate her study habits based on that work. There is an interaction of respect implied in a space like the Quiet Chamber. Such a respect for learning ought to be engendered in all schools.

The Studios

Think of the Studios as places where people go to record and practice performances. Because we should expect many young learners to lean toward the performing arts in choosing topics of study—many will study guitar or anime or film as performance media—schools must have places where rehearsals and practices can occur. But as some students will select public service as their topic area, they will also need space to practice delivering a speech or holding a press conference.

Lindsey, who will be involved in collecting video from basketball archives, will use the Studios to edit videos of a professional quality. Studios are mandatory in a world where digital technology has allowed nearly everyone with a laptop to turn a room into a dedicated space to make their own music, film, video game, or any kind of artistic expression.

But there are other, equally important, reasons for creating these Studios. One is that Lindsey will need space to record interviews with people of all types of basketball background. Allowing her to reserve a Studio equipped with cameras and recording equipment is essential in allowing a full and critical exploration into her interest. It would be unwise to create a learning paradigm that requests the participation of members of the community and then brings those volunteers to a space that smacks of second-class technology. It is also unfair to Lindsey, who may be seen as less capable even before the engagement begins.

Another reason is the opportunity to practice skills of performance necessary for many aspects of Lindsey's study. She seeks to know basketball better not only because she loves it, but also because she wants to earn her living in some connection to the game. As a sports announcer or commentator, Lindsey will have to develop significant skills as a speaker in front of the camera or on the radio, skills that require two very different vocal qualities.

The school must supply opportunities for her to hone those skills. These Studios are places where she could access a ball game from the NCAA archives and then, with a camera on her, rehearse play-by-play analysis of the game in virtual time. Afterward, she could reflect on her performance—in writing for part of her English evaluation—on her skills. These Studios will provide for all three active learning paradigms in ways that clearly help in the development of learning skills.

As with the other learning spaces, the Studio staff needs to be well-selected, so having teachers with significant experience in digital recording will be important. But as with the Quiet Study Centers (discussed later), these Studios will also utilize the growing expertise of students to train other students on the equipment. Because students will choose these areas for personal exploration, there will certainly be students who understand the skills of film editing, audio recording, and mixed-digital media and can serve as demonstrators for those students who use the media as a secondary learning process.

Lindsey will need to work with many different tools while honing the more important skills of verbal fluency, either with a player or about the game. Thus it may not be necessary that she always has a teacher as instructor in these Studios; a qualified student could serve her well. The school should be developing individuals with growing scales of expertise, and these learners will be quite valuable in helping students do the work of their study.

Student Choice Curriculum will be interactive in myriad ways that contemporary education fails to engage. Yet contemporary life engages interactive collaboration in that many of us are or know people who have made their own CD or their own film with software and a laptop. All it took was the help of a few friends, some time, and patience. Moving this kind of cooperative learning into the schools where it will be overseen by a set of media experts as well as by teachers who understand the nature of human learning can only enhance the outcomes for students like Lindsey.

Quiet Study Centers

The Quiet Study Centers will be very similar to current public school media centers. Here are books and magazines and other print resources. Specialists on research skills work here. The Quiet Study Center hosts a battalion of computers, all of which connect to printers. This is where Lindsey goes when she knows she must dig in deeper than her own computer skills allow, for she knows that several teachers there can help her in an instant. This understanding, the need of significant help, is central to Student Choice Curriculum's purpose.

One thing modern technology has created in our students' minds is that all they need to do is an internet search for their question and the right answer will appear, on their laptop, on their phone, or any of the devices they are using that day. They feel all answers are at their fingertips. But a truth of technology is that a broad range of search efficacy exists in computer users, generally delivering a less-than-adequate result in needed information. As is true for all skills, qualities of online research can be improved and honed for myriad tasks; if the goal is to do quality research, there is a good deal to learn beyond what an individual can muster through self-study.

The Quiet Study Centers will be a major focus for all students at different times during their explorations. As with the other centers, students must attend particular and general sessions to learn the skills that quality research entails. We have become a do-it-yourself culture, and many people feel they have a grasp on knowledge acquisition when, in fact, they do not. Students can be the most blatant pretenders here as their natural tendency to embrace digital media makes them appear to be adept at its uses.

However, they still need significant instruction in many aspects of digital research. Moreover, a requirement of Student Choice Curriculum will be that students must be capable of teaching research skills to other students, and thus will be required to demonstrate both the knowledge and the abilities gleaned in the Quiet Study Centers to real learners. Schedules will be strictly enforced, and students will discover quickly that every week will include time spent in the Quiet Study Centers in order to meet a very significant requirement of hours on task in developing research skills. This is a major part of learning how to learn.

Staffing these centers will be specialists in the media sciences, teachers who know how to use the internet effectively and critically. There will always be at least three media specialists on staff for every five hundred students. Because contemporary society is morphing into a world that needs to be savvy with technology, and because technology is changing so quickly that such savvy is impossible for most people save for a few digital geeks, schools must become more aggressive in presenting proper use and critique of the internet.

These skills should be requirements for graduation, something Student Choice Curriculum defines as the time when a learner demonstrates pertinent and transferrable skills that will allow her to join the "real world" within her particular interest area.

Thinking populations are needed, people who know the difference between constructed propaganda and established science. Not everybody is a whiz on the computer, and many defer to youth when elements of technology become a central need. But even the most technically skilled students do not know how to assess the quality of data or websites. Thus, when confronted with information that must be juxtaposed or assimilated to be understood, they are unsure not only how to do the mental work but also how to find the resources that will help them understand the concepts at hand. That's a bad omen for a world so quickly becoming digital.

Quiet Study Centers get their name from the places where "Marion the Librarian" would shush you if you were speaking too loudly. I suspect they will work best when mostly quiet and when students are properly focused. But because of the teaching that will occur there—specialists modeling research skills; and students demonstrating basic techniques of web use—there should always be a low buzz of voices in the air.

Collaborative Workspaces

When you think of Collaborative Workspaces, think of small bands rehearsing their art and of think-tank boards developing their positions. These learning spaces allow students who are doing the same work to come together and share ideas and processes. Of course, "the same work" is a phrase of variable meaning. It may be that several students are exploring the history of drug laws in America, perhaps as a connection to the current issue of legalizing marijuana or perhaps through an understanding of how race plays a role in the creation of laws in our country.

They may be exploring this concept through the lens of music (drugs as muse), medicine (alternative pharmaceuticals), or even religious practice (hallucinogens as ritual). Those students would be doing "the same work" in this learning space. Equally, several students, like Lindsey, may need to learn the skills of interviewing, though through entirely different contexts. As has been noted, Lindsey plans to interview locals who have a notable knowledge of basketball.

Another student, investigating the nature of local immigration, will engage with families of many backgrounds. A student exploring journalism will also need these skills. Putting those three students together to discuss the dilemmas and solutions they have encountered in their study would create a valuable learning experience.

Generally speaking, it will be the teachers staffing the learning centers who make the biggest difference in the quality of the work there, so imagine diverse thinkers who can see the linkage between process and experience that others may not see. For example, I suspect that a learner who is exploring pottery, especially artisan pottery, will be deeply focused on physical techniques, both with the wheel and stationary work, experimenting with hand and finger placement, pressure, and movement.

Such learning might be linked with others who also have physical techniques to explore, like Lindsey, who is dedicating significant time to perfecting her cross-over dribble, the forward and reverse block-out pivot, and the underhand scoop pass. It is probable the potter and the ballplayer will glean a great deal of process information through shared demonstrations and discussions of the skills they are exploring. Repetition and drill can work, but good learners know that personal reflection accompanies practice, and both the potter and the ballplayer may have a great deal to share with each other about insights gained within their physical practice.

Thus Collaborative Workspaces will honor diversity of interactions, with portioned areas that are like the rehearsal spaces mentioned previously but also like the Interactive Construction Arenas described next. Learning environments are always more than physical spaces, something contemporary schools have thought little about. Teachers are put into spaces that do not allow the kinds of interactions needed for the teaching they do. Learning spaces need to inspire; they need to have flexibility so different kinds of engagement can occur frequently.

There should be an intentional collection of art displayed in the Collaborative Workspaces, selected more for its ability to spawn collaborative thought as for its familiarity. Dalí and Miró are probably better choices than Sargent or

Homer, though that won't always be the case. Suffice it to say, Collaborative Workspaces will be places where students know shared thinking will occur.

Interactive Construction Arenas

Interactive Construction Arenas are where frames of mind are built. As with Collaborating Workspaces, here diverse set of students, led by a teacher, explore how they can move their investigations forward. Socratic circles are held here; open forum question-and-answer sessions and collaborative metaphor making are common activities. This is a loud place, a talkative place, where information is shared and brainstorms are welcomed.

Meetings include students who have been pursuing the same, or similar, topics. Lindsey would join others who have chosen basketball, or another sport, as their focus of interest. Since the historic study of basketball would be similar to the historic study of baseball or football or squash, students could discuss how certain perspectives or questions were (or were not) helpful to their exploration. Other elements could be shared in a study of team sports, including: learning the physical skills, rules, and strategies of the game; applying different kinds of statistical data sets used in the game; refining the writing styles used to analyze and describe the game.

Other meetings will include students exploring topics that have no immediate connection to each other, essentially showing that as fields diversify something about pursuits of knowledge in one links meaningfully to pursuits of knowledge in others. Through her study of basketball, Lindsey will discover much about how history uses theories to turn discovered data into knowledge.

When she shares that understanding with a student exploring the internal combustion engine and discovers that this topic, too, offers a plethora of entry points into historiography, she will know better how learning happens. These meetings become important for Student Choice Curriculum's goal of learning how to learn. By placing diverse topics at the same table and then guiding students through critical conversations of method and theory, teachers will show students the plusses and the minuses of specialized knowledge.

Lindsey will present the issues of race and segregation in the NBA, knowing well the problems players faced when the league integrated; but her understanding of those events will be enhanced when a fellow student shares her research on how racial mores played a role when officers at Ellis Island made suggestions and determinations about who would be allowed to enter the United States.

Meetings in the Interactive Construction Arena will be scheduled, and agendas will be set. The point of this learning space is to bring both like and dissimilar minds and projects to the same table to explore knowledge in a more general sense. Such meetings will offer challenges to even the sharpest minds in that they will be placed with students who, perhaps, focused very little on history but a great deal on math, and with another whose focus included a vast exploration of literature though not higher math, and a third whose focus was intensely on early classical art, so a great deal of history but no complex science.

In these meetings, rather than just unpacking the methods and functions of her study, Lindsey will be asked to apply gained knowledge about fields she didn't cover, thus demonstrating her ability to communicate new knowledge clearly, as well as her understanding of what her focus needs to be when presenting information to a less-informed but certainly capable audience. In other words, these engagements will be epistemological in scope, designed to move students beyond the "whats," and onto the "whys" and "hows" of knowing.

Staff at the Interactive Construction Arenas will need to be well prepared to take conversations in multiple directions and to moderate groups so all students supply significant input and ask thoughtful questions. Each meeting in the Interactive Construction Arena will be followed by the assignment of a significant reflection on the nature of the knowledge explored, covering both content and methodology, so attention to the details of the talk will be mandatory.

The room itself need not be ornate, though it should be large enough so several meetings can occur at once. Students should be encouraged to observe some meetings to prepare for their own. This part of Student Choice Curriculum will be one of the demonstration sessions in those first three weeks where all students are invited to observe what will be asked of them as they matriculate through the program.

Think of Interactive Construction Arenas as the place where Lindsey will show peers how and why she has done what she done, as well as what she has discovered through exploring her topic. During these meetings she is open to any and all questions from the students and the teacher at the table. These are a highly demanding set of challenges, and there should be several of them yearly.

THE ATTITUDE OF STUDENT CHOICE CURRICULUM

Aside from reimagining the physical space, there will have to be a significant attitude change on the part of the staff and the administration as well as in the student body in order for Student Choice Curriculum to succeed. The student change will come more quickly, as the opportunity to select and design a personal exploration of interest will be met with welcoming minds. For the staff and administration, the buy-in may be more difficult.

Teachers, even in these years of overwhelming control by legislative and administrative bodies, have been the monarchs of their classrooms, with an unwritten permission to close their doors and teach as they wish. They have designed units and assessment strategies; in many cases they have selected much of the source material to be covered; and they have determined the success or failure of the students under their care. By individualizing most of the educational process, Student Choice Curriculum will change a good deal of that, and such changes do not come easily.

The administration, too, will find the new system to be a difficult transition. High schools move students from buses to classes, from classes to other classes, from classes to lunch and back again, and from classes to buses; all of this will have to be redesigned school by school depending on myriad factors at each school.

The bells that toll classes to an end will have to change to some other system. Students will walk the hallways on their own volition, following up on preset appointments at the Quiet Study Centers or the Interactive Construction Arenas, or arriving at the Studios and Collaborative Workspaces in a punctual fashion. The freedom afforded students in Student Choice Curriculum will push some administrative teams to the brink of frustration as issues like tardiness or skipping essentially disappear.

Students will (still) linger in the hallways, dragging their feet to their next class, but there won't be the opportunity to ask them the question, "Where are you supposed to be right now?" in the same way as before. No set, period-by-period schedule will be given to a Student Choice Curriculum student. Missed appointments will be significant infractions, just as they are in the real world, but the businesslike manner by which schools keep attendance on a daily basis will need to change significantly. These are major issues of the conversations that must be held.

Teachers' daily functions will change, too, though for most this change may be easier to take, because it will emphasize the interest and expertise they bring to the classroom. Michelle might be one of the lucky teachers who work with Lindsey in her study of basketball, as she is a lover of the game, with a significant sense of its heritage. She should find in Lindsey a willingness to explore basketball in a deeper way than even she thought possible, and a few months into her studies they might find themselves looking at philosophies of competition or game theory that come from a win-win rather than win-lose perspective.

Michelle (and Marcus) may find that in the mix of students they serve (yes, Student Choice Curriculum teachers will be responsible for a "standard" amount of students) several are of the kind who allow them to play with ideas they truly love, the kind that always make learning fun. In other words, in Student Choice Curriculum, teachers get to be the experienced learners who are sought out by the novices who, hopefully, truly want to learn more about something they already love.

Of course, there will be chaos. Days will not be of the seven-period type where one period is for planning and a lunch period sits nicely between two classes. Rather, teachers will have to make schedules and share experiences with others in ways that make Monday look and behave nothing like Tuesday which is so dissimilar from Wednesday that you might not believe they are all days of the same week. But those differences in day-to-day life will make Student Choice Curriculum schools more like the work people do in the "real world."

Academic departments will have to determine how subject information will be taught in direct instruction classes that still exist, some for Student Choice students and some for those who did not (or would not) create their learning plan. Some teachers may want only to teach Student Choice or non–Student Choice classes, and in some schools that may work fine. Some schools may opt for all teachers taking part in direct instruction so that no one class of students is served by only one teacher in that subject all year.

In other words, every class becomes a seminar of sorts, where shared expertise is the name of the game. Imagine the positive outcomes when Lindsey sees a friend in the Interactive Construction Arena and begs her to come to her journalism tutorial because the woman who teaches that class is just so engaging that no one ought to go through high school without having at least one class from her.

These attitudinal changes will come hard, if only because schools and their systems are so entrenched that it is difficult to imagine them any other way. If a coach has been using a three-quarter court zone trap for the last two seasons, with players who are coming back for another year, and she tries to shift those players to a man-to-man full-court press, she had better get her attitude shifted or she and the players will scurry back to the zone trap after the first game when they get beaten down the floor by a weaker team.

There will be lots of obstacles to implementing Student Choice Curriculum, and each day the working staff will learn something they needed to know the day before. But if the staff is brave and thoughtful, creative and cooperative, they will overcome the obstacles they face, for education is often its own reward, and such a system as Student Choice Curriculum offers the potential for the greatest reward: students who learn and who know what learning is.

THIS MAY BE EXPENSIVE

There should be little doubt that this program will be expensive, and the cost of education will rise. Moreover, school-by-school enrollment will have to be smaller, as no highly effective education—Student Choice Curriculum or the traditional, contemporary education presently being offered—can work with the numbers of students we place in so many of our schools.

Evolutionary psychologist Robin Dunbar, in some significant comparative primate studies in the 1980s, calculated correlations between brain size with group size in nonhuman primates. Using data from those studies, Dunbar speculated that the size of the human brain indicates we should live in groups that number between 150 to 200 individuals, maximum. This would allow us the social contact and rich personal knowledge needed for group and kinship survival. Such data hold up when we measure contemporary nomadic, hunter-gatherer groups. They also seem to account for circles of influence within friendship patterns.

Thus, Student Choice Curriculum, in typical high schools, should enroll somewhere between 450 and 700 students, based on Dunbar's numbers per year in the program. For sure this will mean creating many schools-within-a-school experiences. Schools may never get to what Dunbar's data show, but shifting to schools of seven hundred or less at least acknowledges how data on human group size could matter in improving education. Learning is social; learners must know their learning peers; schools must be smaller.

Schools of the kind being described here become the hub of their community. They create more civic energy than they use; they are places where the community comes together for many important functions. Schools that are more elaborate in design as well as more efficient in function could be used for much more than just the school day; they would become a place of growth for their community.

DOUBLING DOWN ON THE MAJOR ISSUES

1. A visit to most high schools in the United States will reveal learning spaces that are outdated, both in function and form.
2. Learning spaces help in the motivational process, so they need to be reimagined, even personified, to invite thoughtful, collaborative work.
3. Well-conceived learning spaces create significantly richer intellectual investment.

4. Learning spaces should inspire: work with those who share interests; work with those of a different interest. Learning spaces in Student Choice Curriculum should be designed to help students understand how to learn.
5. Elements of Student Choice Curriculum schools should be repurposed so community events regularly occur there.
6. In Student Choice Curriculum, teachers get to showcase their expertise on the nature of learning with students who are learning what it means to learn and who seek that end.
7. Much of what schools do—bells, hallways, lunches, assemblies—can be stressful for many students, so care must be given to creating spaces that reduce stress.
8. Much in Student Choice Curriculum will be student driven, so many skills will be taught/modeled by other students as a part of their evaluation process.
9. Student Choice Curriculum *must be* carried out in smaller schools. This may mean many schools-within-a-school situations, though individual stand-alone schools are better.

Chapter 6

Education Is Democratic

The surest way to corrupt a young man is to teach him to esteem more highly those who think alike than those who think differently.

—Nietzsche

FRAMING THOUGHTS

Certainly, ideas of freedom matter to all human beings, and for those who experience it, freedom is one of the great joys of life. But to what extent do you make the connection between freedom and the design of an effective education? While you move toward the end of this text, consider how your own education was focused through "freedom to" or "freedom from," and evaluate how that may have mattered to the outcomes you attained. As you read, explore the link you make between learning and life, and perhaps return to the opening of this book and the idea that personal interest may have motivated some of your most recent learning engagements. To what degree might that kind of learning promote individual freedom more than, say, institutional learning? Then finally ponder what role students should play in their own learning—should they choose or be directed toward the topics that frame their curricular studies?

There are many reasons why Student Choice Curriculum would be better than present methods of educating our students, some dealing with the nature of learning, some focused on the implementation of the curriculum, and some steeped in basic human rights. Education enhances critical thought, which engenders the freedom to act intentionally toward a better life. Education promotes freedom as a goal of civilization. It explores the nature of freedom in its dual context of freedom to and freedom from. It is difficult to speak of freedom without considering both sides of that coin.

Certainly, as Americans, we are aware the Second Amendment provides the freedom to purchase and carry a firearm; but rights of privacy and property also guarantee safety from someone using that firearm improperly. Analogously, we can't talk about education without considering both the opportunities and the limitations—the freedoms of learning—it provides to students. Students should be *freed from* unnecessary curricular requirements so they can be freed to learn well and deeply. Much of what is required in our schools holds little value for most individuals in our society.

Contemporary life demonstrates the fallacy that most individuals need Algebra II or higher levels of math to function. Millions of people whose math skills do not extend beyond addition, subtraction, multiplication, and division do quite well in the United States; to demand of high school students that they must know more to graduate is misguided. Equally nonproductive are requirements of multiple years of a single science or history. Certainly we want students to have significant knowledge in these subject areas, but to coerce them to complete unnecessary learning challenges is tantamount to malpractice.

A student only benefits from three years of history or science when that student sees a reason to take those particular courses. Otherwise, the time in those classrooms and labs is little more than tedium. Of course, no student who dreams of becoming an engineer of any type should be denied the opportunity to study mathematics at a very high level; she should also take physics classes as often as she wishes.

Freeing students from the unproven mandates of required courses is a central reason to incorporate Student Choice Curriculum, which will work to provide and allow rather than to require and limit.

In turn, students should be *freed to* make significant decisions about the education they receive. They should pick subject areas and resources, as well as set their own goals for academic and intellectual exploration. Such decisions will engage them in studies that develop learning skills they can take with them when they leave high school. If a student wants to become an anthropologist or an event coordinator, she should not have to wait until college to begin guided studies in those fields. Schools should free students to turn their interests into curricular scaffolding.

For education to provide opportunities for positive and successful futures, the learner must be present and active in all decisions that create that future. For too long schools have dictated what hoops students must jump through before they get to play in the "real world." Students should be allowed to imagine their own hoops through which they can jump. Of course, those jumps may need the guidance and oversight of a teacher who has already made the leap, but that only serves to exemplify the importance of the learning relationships Student Choice Curriculum hopes to engender.

This book has continually encouraged that readers begin significant conversations about Student Choice Curriculum, conversations that should be steeped in the ideas of positive and negative freedom. With good clear thinking in the forefront of these conversations, more reasons for creating schools of Student Choice Curriculum will emerge.

ACADEMIC BUY-IN

Student Choice Curriculum will create buy-in of the educational process for nearly all students; many more will begin to like school in ways that does not happen today. This attitude should not be downplayed. Education benefits when people connect with its goals and processes, and if more students found the process to be enjoyable, more schools would become friendlier and more effective centers of learning. If a generation of students enjoyed their K–12 experience, they'd do a great deal in seeing that their kids liked it too. That momentum would be a boon for our culture, as it would probably make many people take education more seriously.

One of the major sticking points of America's educational system is that students see no good reasons for bringing what they learn into their lives. Institutional learning and life are not linked in our students' understanding of the world. They may recite the mantra, "to get a good job get a good education," but they do not understand how good jobs are functions of good societies or how well-educated people work together to build the systems needed for societal progress.

Students are not asked to probe and evaluate elements of their own communities even as parts of their towns thrive or die; they are not asked to speculate on the nature of how innovations cause societies to change and then how such changes affect the citizens who live there. Consequently, students never engage in any kind of real-time application of skills that might demonstrate how learning is linked to the lives they live. Rather they are merely asked to learn facts or formulae and then apply them to standardized challenges.

Contemporary students hold little appreciation for the knowledge owned by a good reader or demonstrated by the conversationalist who understands the ebb and flow of general and specific history. Students may recite the social and political causes that brought about World War I, though not in any historically functional way. Too many students cannot connect those events to the political world they should call home; and they rarely see how the novels of, say, Steinbeck might be instrumental in understanding civil rights elements of our current world.

But were schools to allow students to play a major role in their learning, the kind of role Student Choice Curriculum encourages, clever and creative teachers could help them see how a novel or a moment in history or a scientific discovery fits intricately with their chosen interest. Thus, students would start to make the connections that unite experience and education.

Learning needs to touch lives and activate minds in ways that reveal to the learner the fit and function of the real world. By allowing students to choose their path of study, Student Choice Curriculum would help students see the cause and effect of learning's purpose. Humans learn so they can apply critical thought to the problems that befall their lives. They think critically to move beyond the dilemmas and toward systems that make life more functional, better. Student Choice Curriculum could be instrumental in showing students that the learning process is valuable for both the individual and the society.

THE DEMANDS OF DEMOCRACY

This points to another central reason for transitioning current educational paradigms to Student Choice Curriculum: democracy demands it. America's core belief that all people are endowed with certain unalienable rights of life, liberty, and the pursuit of happiness is diminished by not allowing students to pursue and internalize those rights within the institutional world of education. Indeed, to place upon students a set of curricular mandates and standards that disallow open choice is tantamount to treason.

Our current educational practices, deliberately and with aforethought, confine young minds to the shackles of noncreative thought and expression in the guise of shaping them for our culture. Schools teach them to toe the line and become automatons in the corporate capitalist structure that needs them only to be consumers and (only then) workers. Everything about a school is tit-for-tat in structure. Wear these uniforms, be on time, do your work, and get into a good college. The trouble is, students get no say in either side of that bargain.

Our educational practices rob students of the ability to develop the kind of thought that led our ancestors to fight for the freedoms we hold sacred. There is nothing democratic in asking Lindsey to complete so much math, so much science, and so much history in order to graduate from high school. There is nothing democratic in forcing her to attain performance levels for tasks in which she will find no real-world application. There is nothing democratic in textbooks that neglect to account for the lived experience of real people who go about life daily trying to find and to make meaning from a complex world that has not treated them fairly.

Orwell said those who control the past control the present, and we are doing very little to instill in our students the values that might make them appreciate either and to gain some control over their own lives. Democracy cannot stand without educated minds, as it is a forward-moving, progressive force that always seeks better ways of life, fortifying equality and constantly adding opportunities for all citizens.

Every time some new group is allowed to enjoy rights it had been denied previously, American democracy is strengthened.

Every time a new person is granted opportunities of citizenship, to take part in the community of the American spirit, American democracy is strengthened.

If students, as individuals and as a group, should be allowed new freedoms in determining the nature of the education they receive, democracy will be strengthened.

But presently, rigid restrictions of curricular mandates, emphasized in programs like Common Core, No Child Left Behind, and Race to the Top, prevent students from experiencing education as a life-changing and affirming process. Rather than being treated like free-minded individuals, they experience school as if indentured servants.

If America's educational system hopes to prepare citizens to play a role in a government of the people, by the people, and for the people, then it needs to become a system that is of the student, by the student, and for the student.

There are many ways to accomplish this task, and Student Choice Curriculum is only one of them; but considering more recent trends in education, moves that have been more autocratic than democratic, it is essential our nation move steadily and robustly—and quickly!—in a direction that dignifies the dreams and desires as well as the abilities and aptitudes of our learners.

Student Choice Curriculum provides a robust and rigorous nature that could turn education directly toward democratic practices. Once present in our schools, its rich interactive learning engagements will help engender the conversations and critical evaluations of myriad cultural behaviors.

WHAT IT MEANS FOR EDUCATION

Many, both inside and out of education, will ask how choice equals democracy. I am tempted to borrow from Louis Armstrong's reply to a fan who asked Satchmo, "What is jazz?"

"If you have to ask what jazz is," Armstrong said, "you'll never know."

If you're wondering, after reading this book, what Student Choice Curriculum has to do with reforming education, you may never really understand it at all. Of course, that belittles both the misunderstanding and the nature of a book that seeks to detail the importance of a new system. Forget Satchmo for a moment.

What else can Student Choice Curriculum do for education?

American democracy promises that an individual who works hard with a firm purpose and a sense of self-betterment will find ultimate success, liberty, and happiness. American democracy believes people should find work to be self-fulfilling, identity building, and a place to turn toward when life knocks them down hard. When times are difficult, American workers often believe a second job might help them through, and they don't hesitate to seek it.

People's belief in American democracy provides incentive for many to push themselves beyond their limits. Choice is a key to this thinking. Americans choose to take part in the American Dream, choose to better themselves through all sorts of practices, one of which is learning. The nation so believed in the power of education that after World War II, the GI Bill allowed for veterans to go to college or trade schools on stipends or grants. The government provided the money, and the vet chose his (nearly always "his" at that time) own path of progress.

American democracy promises each individual a chance to shape her own life and direct her own pursuit of liberty and happiness. What she does in the freedom of her mind and dreams is sacrosanct as it helps her create her own world.

We have decided she can marry whom she loves, so we should allow her to study what she wishes.

We have decided she can worship in her own way, so we should allow her to explore intellectual topics of her own choice.

We have said she can become as mighty as she wishes, even to serve in the most elite branches of our military, so we should allow her to blaze the educational trail that gives her the most satisfaction.

American democracy promises that all individuals may dream large and freely, feel confident and safe within their own home, and move about their country with assurance that they will be treated as Americans who deserve a place at the decision making table of democracy.

How can we not let our students choose their own adventure in education?

Presently, American education denies choice at nearly every turn. Students are required to complete long lists of courses in order to graduate, and within each of those courses come a litany of "required readings" or "mandatory projects." To my knowledge there has never been a clear demonstration of a real-life advantage in completing the mathematics or history or science or literature demanded in our graduation requirements. That these courses make someone generally smarter may be true, but nothing has ever shown them to be a sufficient condition to the good life.

Anyone who has made a career teaching high school English knows the joy of reading Shakespeare or Eliot or Woolf or García Márquez. But they also know it matters little what Lindsey reads so long she reads often and with a curious and probing, intentional mind. If Macbeth, Banquo, Duncan, and Macduff demonstrate how the lessons of power and corruption and a flawed inner nature are central to understanding significant aspects of human experience, so too can Voldemort, Snape, Dumbledore, and Harry Potter when the reader is thoughtful and the conversations are rich.

Shakespeare leaves many high school students, and many adults, wondering why so much attention is paid to his collected works. Aside from *Romeo and Juliet*, his stories do not focus on young minds making decisions. Most of Shakespeare's themes and tales are understood best only after significant life experiences. Some students explore and embrace the humanity found in Shakespeare's poetics, and they should be allowed that choice. But many more students would be better served through readings of their own choice, provided those texts were treated in ways that made serious the themes and conflicts found on their pages.

Don't miss the point: Student Choice Curriculum is not about avoiding key issues or works in developing young minds. It is just that the issues students need to wrap their heads around might be better served through entry points already available to those students. If someone is of the mind that the struggle of race in America is worth a great deal of attention in our high schools, educators everywhere would agree.

However, if that same someone claimed race could not be well understood through the plights of Jackie Robinson, Nate "Sweetwater" Clifton, or Curt Flood, they would be wrong. They would not understand the way individual human minds interact with pertinent knowledge, nor would they appreciate how personal interest engenders the application of mental work to an issue like race. Allowing Lindsey to choose her area of interest provides an invitation for deep exploration into issues that our current pedagogical approaches leave students nonplussed.

One reason for transforming education into Student Choice Curriculum is to engender in learners the idea that connections matter and are instructive; that each learner already possesses a significant entry point to complex topics. When Lindsey finds that her world of interest has a history framed in part by racism, she will dig deeper and discover more. Moreover, she will be ready and willing to act with the new knowledge she gains, taking it with her when she leaves the learning environment. At all levels of life, learning is more portable when it fits into our repertoire of interest; there is no reason for this to be different with high school students.

That there are good reasons for students to be mindful of science and mathematics is undeniable, but when we see daily how a whole group of politicians and corporate leaders lack sophistication for the science of global climate change, evolution, and sexual-orientation variability, we must question the manner by which we have taught those subjects over the years. Had these leaders been allowed to explore science through a chosen personal interest, their understanding of the field would be clearer and, potentially, more ethical (though the partisan nature of capitalist politics tells me these leaders might not make different decisions).

None of what education presents scientifically to our students is making them any better at understanding how human influence on global climate change is putting the world at tremendous risk; none of the history helps our students understand how America's racism is still a major force not only in our communities but also in our governmental policies; and none of what we are doing mathematically is helping our students understand the distribution of wealth and the real problems perpetrated by the gap between the haves and have-nots of our country, something nearly all economists point to as a significant problem for our near future.

If none of the classes or courses currently offered are making our students smarter about the ills we face as a nation and a planet, if education is not helping our society find new ways of addressing those ills head-on, then it is neither serving its central purpose nor is it being democratic. Thus, it becomes our duty to change it.

By definition, democracy is an active form of government, where it behooves all involved to be attentive to situations and conditions on both a local and national scale. As Rousseau states, "When the citizens . . . love repose more than freedom," the state may not have long to survive. Thus, schools ought to be places where students learn the methods of public action and discourse, where they are allowed to investigate and imagine different methods and outcomes for their world.

There is no better way to accomplish this than to allow them to choose what they will study and then direct them toward avenues of interaction within those issues. When Lindsey chooses what she'll study, she will be reinforced in the idea that democracy is, foundationally, a citizen-run enterprise. When she is allowed to choose what she'll study, she will be the one who holds herself accountable to the learning she must demonstrate to fulfill graduation requirements. Thus she will learn of citizen responsibility.

When Lindsey is allowed to explore basketball in all aspects of the curriculum, she and her teachers have a better chance to see what learning can accomplish in the right circumstances. Student Choice Curriculum will encourage Lindsey to see herself as a learner, a seeker who must know how, when, and why to bring certain skills and cognitive functions to the task of learning. It will be a way for her to understand that upon graduation, she can not only demonstrate her skills as a problem-solver, but she will know how to continue to improve those skills on her own, over the time of her life.

American democracy, at its core, suggests that if the marketplace of ideas is opened to myriad minds who think deeply and critically about the issues of the time, the right idea will rise to the top and show itself to be a superior way to solve or address the problems at hand. Such an understanding of liberty holds that dynamically liberal societies must be bursting with new and divergent concepts at all moments.

Good thinking demands that contrary ideas be brought into the argument of what makes a good life. When we are not seeking ways to stretch the boundaries of freedom or to broaden our understanding of what needs to be done to make the playing field more equitable, we are neither creating nor dignifying liberty. Democracy and liberty should welcome new ideas as opportunities to dream about futures not yet experienced and to evaluate a present that does (and does not) accomplish certain goals. Presently, none of this attains any significant outcomes in our present educational systems.

Our top-loaded set of requirements posits a singular mind coming from our schools, not a multivariate assortment of thinkers who enjoy the give-and-take of open debate. Schools ask that everyone take the same courses and then pass the same tests, which is no way to engender diverse frames of mind or new avenues of debate.

If we are not putting big ideas in front of our students, if we are not giving them the opportunity to debate openly the merits of single-payer health-care systems or the legalization of marijuana or the rights of all to live and marry freely and express their desires by voting, including former felons, then we are not serving the metaphor of the marketplace of ideas in our schools. If we are not encouraging our students to look deeply into that which interests them in order to find a way to construct their own life and well-being, we are not providing them opportunities to understand the American dream on a personal level.

American democracy suggests that of all the privileges we have, the most sacred is the ability to speak openly about any and all topics. If our students are not allowed to select their own course of study, if they do not have a say in how they will learn and be evaluated and move forward intellectually, they are not being provided with that most-cherished freedom. Thus, they cannot know or understand its inherent power.

Lindsey should know that she can connect herself to the things she finds fitting and interesting. She may join any club, read any book, debate any issue, and express herself in myriad ways in the public sphere. Lindsey should know that, provided she hurts no one along the way, her choices are hers to make.

My educational experiences have shown that we no longer discuss with any energy what it means to be an American or a small-d democrat. Education is no longer about the big ideas or the personal identification with normative or alternative ideologies. It is rare today to find students able or willing to speak thoughtfully about communism or socialism or libertarianism, or any of the other -isms that once peppered the conversations I shared with students who were peers and who populated the classes of my early years in the profession.

This ought to raise deep concerns about the direction and content of current educational practices. It must be true that many high school students have a diverse set of feelings and ideas about the systems they see working (and not) in our country. Not to provide them with a venue for sharing and exploring those ideas is counterintuitive to the foundational documents of our nation. Democracy requires citizens to know how the government works; they must know how people think, how they negotiate, how they understand and interact with each other.

To live in a democracy requires citizens to have a sense of the wants and needs of others, especially those others who come from backgrounds so different that few shared cultural practices exist between them. It is not possible to attain equality or liberty without this knowledge; both evolve through the intricate, self-organizing system that is human interaction. Nor is their importance easily learned through didactic lessons, lectures, or by reading a textbook. An understanding of liberty and equality comes only through real-time, face-to-face encounters between stakeholders.

People with a vested interest in what they learn bring to the marketplace of ideas reasons for the qualities they extol. When confronted by others who see things differently, in real-time arguments, they reassess and revise (though maybe not change) their initial concepts. That our nation needs significant lessons on how this works is readily apparent when one stops and considers Charleston, Sutherland Springs, Las Vegas, Parkland, or any other recent shootings. Democracy makes significant demands on its citizens, and when those demands disappear from the educational process, the quality of human life will drop proportionately.

How can we not let our students choose their own adventure in education?

Another important reason for supporting Student Choice Curriculum is that human beings have a common need to be seen, to be acknowledged, and to be valued for the ideas and skills they bring to life. Encouraging students to explore interests and then to bring what they find to the table of authentic assessment is an excellent way for them to be seen not only as doers but also as creators of their own knowledge. This is a highly courageous act.

Within the context of Student Choice Curriculum, students will be continually asked to present their gleanings to "experts" in the worlds they are exploring. Lindsey will develop and deliver many presentations, write many papers, and engage in many significant conversations during her time exploring the game, while connecting it to all things academic. Many of her works will be seen and evaluated by coaches, fans, players, journalists and others who involve themselves with the game at all levels. Consequently, Lindsey will be seen and heard.

In current classroom situations, students can hide from the discussion and thus not learn how to ask pertinent questions. Sometimes, considering how large classes can be, this hiding occurs without teachers noticing. Very little in our current educational practices mandates interactive engagement with authentic audiences. Students can complete four years of high school without being seen as a learner, as a thinker, or as a knower.

Student Choice Curriculum is fashioned around self-created learning experiences that promote interaction with other students, teachers, and authentic audiences to develop communication skills that clarify learning skills, goals, projects, and potential outcomes. A curricular skill set will focus on the reciprocal nature of personal exploration through conversations about chosen topics and the connections that link those topics with the real world of people, politics, and economics. Student Choice Curriculum recognizes that in the complexity of our contemporary global society, messages get muddled for reasons that are correctable.

Consequently, along the educational journey this curriculum offers, teachers and students will make sure that all learners come face-to-face with others who think differently, hold different values, and pursue different ends within the same topic areas. To engage in that kind of ideological difference is to realize how endeavors of excellence often come from (must come from?) disparate goals and frameworks. Learning how to meet those differences head-on and simultaneously derive a set of viable outcomes is paramount to preserving meaningful life.

A nation like ours, multicultural and multiethnic, needs young minds to interact in the freedom of their own creation while in the presence of a diverse set of interlocutors who might help them shape their goals and outcomes accordingly. Today's schooling does little to engender these opportunities, and our schools are often highly self-segregated and cliqued, with the only interactions between divergent groups occurring in the cafeteria or on the athletic fields. Democratizing our schools would do a lot to restart the process of cultural assimilation; it would create opportunities for many to experience how the "other half" thinks, works, and dreams.

How can we not let our students choose their own adventure in education?

This book promotes the idea that we need a significant conversation about Student Choice Curriculum as a potential change agent for our schools. A final reason for this argument is that our world is moving too fast to do otherwise. Schooling just cannot keep up with how quickly new knowledge comes into play for nearly everyone. To keep treating the body of knowledge as something that can be captured and brought to the minds of our K–12 students through clear questioning and dedicated pedagogy is just not reasonable.

By the time one lesson is internalized, another understanding of the same principle, probably deeper and more developed, has taken its place in the world of ideas. As our students learn the technological skills of one application, a new technology eclipses that methodology rendering the old skills—perhaps only months old—obsolete. There is just too much to know and no singular way to determine what things Lindsey will need to be considered ready and able to take part in the modern sense of world building. As Carl Sagan says,

> When the training is unchanged for immense periods of time, traditions are passed on intact to the next generation. But when what needs to be learned changes quickly, especially in the course of a single generation, it becomes much harder to know what to teach and how to teach it. Then, students complain about relevance; respect for their elders diminishes. Teachers despair at how educational standards have deteriorated, and how lackadaisical students have become. In a world in transition, students and teachers both need to teach themselves one essential skill—learning how to learn.

We are absolutely a world in transition. Such a life, for so many of our citizens, comes and goes with no reflective processes, as each new toy seems to be here so quickly that we embrace the new without ever fully having understood the old. Somehow this has to stop, though in a way that progress continues, life moves forward, and humans continue to construct a world in which they can live.

As I understand that dilemma, I see education as the only path that can work, the only way that people can come together and speak of a world that supports life for all. And the only way education can do that is if it dignifies the desires and choices of students and focuses intensely on teaching students how to learn.

Thus in the hopes that this book engenders conversations about education and Student Choice Curriculum all over this land, I ask once again,

How can we not let our students choose their own adventure in education?

DOUBLING DOWN ON THE MAJOR ISSUES

1. Education enhances critical thought, which engenders the freedom to act intentionally toward a better life. Students should be *freed from* unnecessary curricular requirements so they can be *freed to* learn well and deeply.

2. Student Choice Curriculum will work to provide and allow rather than to require and limit.
3. When student interest drives the learning, students will build their own intellectual scaffolding and become the ones who hold themselves accountable for learning, thus directly experiencing citizen responsibility.
4. A generation of learners who enjoyed their K–12 experience would work to encourage their children also to enjoy education. This would be a boon for our culture.
5. Democracy demands that education be of the student, by the student, and for the student if we wish to maintain that all citizens have the rights of life, liberty, and the pursuit of happiness.
6. Because individual minds interact with knowledge stimuli differently, we must create learning spaces that dignify those individual interactions. Student Choice Curriculum can accomplish this.

Selected Bibliography

Bergen, Benjamin. *Louder Than Words: The New Science of How the Brain Makes Meaning*. New York: Basic Books, 2012.
Blum, Deborah. *Love at Goon Park: Harry Harlow and the Science of Affection*. New York: Basic Books, 2002.
Boaler, J., and Pablo Zoido. "Why Math Education in the U.S. Doesn't Add Up." *MIND, Scientific American* 27, no. 6 (November/December 2016): 18, 19.
Bransford, J., A. Brown, and R. Cocking, eds. *How People Learn: Brain, Mind, Experience, and School*. Washington, DC: National Academy Press, 2000.
Bruner, John. *The Culture of Education*. Cambridge, MA: Harvard University Press, 1996.
Darling-Hammond, Linda. *The Right to Learn: A Blueprint for Creating Schools That Work*. San Francisco: Jossey-Bass, 1997.
Dewey, John. *Democracy and Education: An Introduction to the Philosophy of Education*. New York: Free Press, 1944.
———. *How We Think*. Boston: D. C. Heath, 1910.
Dunbar, R. "Coevolution of Neocortical Size, Group Size and Language in Humans." *Behavioral and Brain Sciences* 16, no. 3 (March 1993): 681–735.
Dweck, Carol. *Self-Theories: Their Role in Motivation, Personality, and Development*. Philadelphia: Psychology Press, 2000.
Egan, Kieran. *The Educated Mind: How Cognitive Tools Shape Our Understanding*. Chicago: University of Chicago Press, 1997.
Freire, Paulo. *Pedagogy of Freedom: Ethics, Democracy, and Civic Courage*. Translated by Patrick Clarke. New York: Rowman & Littlefield, 1998.
———. *Pedagogy of the Oppressed*. Translated by Patrick Clarke. New York: Continuum International, 1970.
Gardner, Howard. *The Unschooled Mind: How Children Think and How Schools Should Teach*. New York: Basic Books, 1991.
Huxley, Aldous. *Island*. New York: Harper Perennial, 1962.

Klingberg, Torkel. *The Learning Brain: Memory and Brain Development in Children.* New York: Oxford University Press, 2013.
Mitra, Dana. "The Social and Economic Benefits of Public Education." Accessed April 2013. White Paper on Public Education. https://www.elc-pa.org/wp-content/uploads/2011/06/BestInvestment_Full_Report_6.27.11.pdf.
Noddings, Nel. *Happiness and Education.* Cambridge: Cambridge University Press, 2003.
Pollan, Michael. *In Defense of Food: An Eater's Manifesto.* New York: Penguin Press, 2008.
Ravitch, Diane. *Reign of Error: The Hoax of the Privatization Movement and the Danger to America's Public Schools.* New York: Alfred A. Knopf, 2013.
Ripley, Amanda. *The Smartest Kids in the World: And How They Got That Way.* New York: Simon & Schuster, 2013.
Robinson, Ken. *Out of Our Minds: Learning to be Creative.* Chester, West Sussex, UK: Capstone Publishing, 2001.
Rorty, Richard. *Philosophy and the Mirror of Nature.* Princeton, NJ: Princeton University Press, 1979.
Rousseau, Jean-Jacques. *The Social Contract.* Baltimore: Penguin Books, 1968.
Sagan, Carl. *The Demon-Haunted World: Science as a Candle in the Dark.* New York: Random House, 1996.
Skrtic, Thomas, ed. *Disability and Democracy: Reconstructing (Special) Education for Postmodernity.* New York: Teacher's College Press, 1995.
Stone-Wiske, Martha, ed. *Teaching for Understanding*: *Linking Research with Practice.* San Francisco: Jossey-Bass, 1998.
Swartz, Barry. "The Paradox of Choice." Filmed 2005 at TEDGlobal. Video, 18:22. https://www.ted.com/talks/barry_schwartz_on_the_paradox_of_choice/transcript#t-60095.
Tippett, Krista. "The Poetry of Creatures." In *Becoming Wise: An Inquiry into the Mystery and Art of Living*, 15–56. New York: Penguin Books, 2017.
Twain, Mark. *The Adventures of Tom Sawyer.* New York: Penguin Classics, 1986.
Vygotsky, L. *Mind and Society: The Development of Higher Psychological Processes.* Cambridge, MA: Harvard University Press, 1978.

About the Author

Ben Graffam currently teaches Theory of Knowledge and philosophy at International Baccalaureate East in Haines City, Florida. Since beginning as an educator in 1982, he has earned a master's degree in gifted education and a PhD in special education, taught gifted studies at the University of South Florida's (USF) College of Education, and served as an education specialist at USF's College of Medicine. His research has been published in journals of both gifted and medical education. He lives in Lakeland, Florida, with his wife, Cheryl, and their cats, Tawny and Ruby, the Port Sisters.

www.ingramcontent.com/pod-product-compliance
Lightning Source LLC
Chambersburg PA
CBHW030114010526
44116CB00005B/238